• HALSGROVE DISCOVER SERIES ➤

LAND'S END

WALKING THE CORNISH COAST FROM ST IVES TO ST MICHAEL'S MOUNT

OLIVER HAWKER

HALSGROVE

First published in Great Britain in 2003

Title page photograph: *Cape Cornwall.*

British Library Cataloguing-in-Publication Data
A CIP record for this title is available from the British Library

The author and publisher strongly recommend the use of the appropriate OS maps
when attempting to walk the South West Coast Path.

ISBN 1 84114 258 1

HALSGROVE

Halsgrove House
Lower Moor Way
Tiverton, Devon EX16 6SS
Tel: 01884 243242
Fax: 01884 243325
email: sales@halsgrove.com
website: www.halsgrove.com

Printed and bound by D'Auria Industrie Grafiche Spa, Italy

Sennen Cove seen from the beach.

For Cherry

It is not England.
It is bare and climated. Tristian's Land.
I lie looking down at a cove
where the waves come while under a low headland
which slopes up in bare green brown, bare
and sad under a level sky.
It is old Celtic — pre Christian.

D H Lawrence

CONTENTS

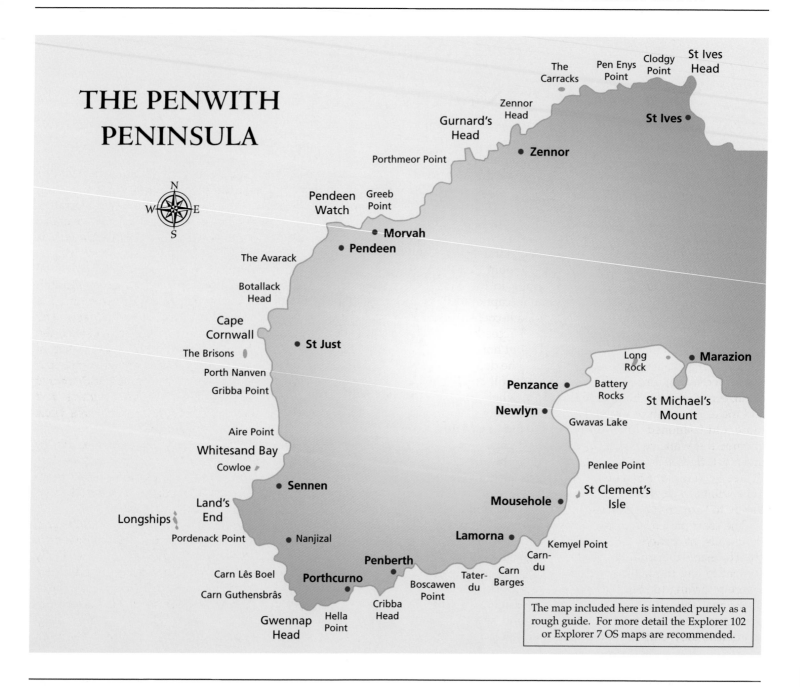

THE PENWITH PENINSULA

St Ives Head
Clodgy Point
Pen Enys Point
The Carracks
Zennor Head
St Ives
Gurnard's Head
Zennor
Porthmeor Point
Pendeen Watch
Greeb Point
Morvah
Pendeen
The Avarack
Botallack Head
Cape Cornwall
St Just
The Brisons
Porth Nanven
Gribba Point
Long Rock
Marazion
Penzance
Battery Rocks
St Michael's Mount
Newlyn
Gwavas Lake
Aire Point
Whitesand Bay
Cowloe
Penlee Point
St Clement's Isle
Sennen
Land's End
Mousehole
Longships
Lamorna
Kemyel Point
Pordenack Point
Nanjizal
Carn-du
Carn Lês Boel
Penberth
Carn Barges
Porthcurno
Tater-du
Carn Guthensbrâs
Boscawen Point
Cribba Head
Gwennap Head
Hella Point

The map included here is intended purely as a rough guide. For more detail the Explorer 102 or Explorer 7 OS maps are recommended.

INTRODUCTION

I've written this book because I love walking. I also love photography and I really love history, British history in particular. The coast path has, during the six years I've lived in Cornwall, provided me with the opportunity to indulge myself in all three.

I originally intended the book to be a pictorial essay of the walk between St Ives and St Michael's Mount, but as I sat down in the Morrab Road reference library in Penzance and began a little light research for picture captions, it soon dawned on me that pretty pictures with half-cocked explanations beneath them could have only ever succeeded in telling a fraction of a fraction of the story. So I went home and had a think. Here is the result. It is by no means the definitive study of the peninsula; what I've omitted would fill another book again, but I believe, I hope, it will serve to whet your appetite and make you want to don a pair of sturdy boots, buy one of those old-fashioned long stick things and a jumper, and attempt the walk yourself. Within these pages you will be given a little insight into a lot, rather than be subjected to a degree-level dissertation on a little, if you catch my drift. The onus will then be on you to explore further when, and if, you decide to take up the challenge laid down and walk the path.

The coast path around the Penwith peninsula is walked by thousands of people every year; some attempt the entire stretch, using the walk as a holiday in itself, while most are content to join the path at various points and walk for a day before returning to base. There are many pocket-sized guide books available which provide a limited insight into what the path has to offer, covering contemporary and historical points of interest, local watering holes and camp-sites, etc. The idea behind this book, however, is to give an insight into West Penwith as a whole, with the path serving as a connecting highway, not only in the physical sense, but also as a narrative link between the huge diversity of subjects the book covers.

The path is a highway which, at any time, allows the walker to take the next exit and explore the world around its fringes. The entire spectrum of the natural and human history of the peninsula can be appreciated by the walk; it passes through almost all the major human settlements of the region and it is within these that the 'meat-and-two-veg' of the book lies. The history of fishing, the establishment of the art colonies, the construction of the lighthouses, the triumphs and disasters of the tin-mining industry, the trials and tribulations of civil and international wars, the granting of the harbour and market charters, pirates, smugglers and excise men, legends and superstitions, and famous wreckings and rescues; this book will give the reader an insight into them all.

The description of the walk itself is by no means highly detailed. I'm not expecting people to carry this book as they scramble over stiles and across rock pools, using it as a step-by-step guide to the next headland or village. The descriptions do, however, assume you will be doing the walk.

The history of all the major settlements – St Ives, Zennor, Morvah, St Just, Sennen, Porthgwarra, Porthcurno, Penberth, Lamorna, Mousehole, Newlyn, Penzance and eventually Marazion and the Mount itself – have been included, for within lies the very essence of West Cornwall. In these hamlets, villages and towns, lie some remarkable stories involving such diverse characters as artists, miners, smugglers, lifeboat men, chartists, soldiers, fishermen, farmers, philanthropists, politicians, dukes, duchesses, kings, queens, landlords, Cavaliers, Roundheads, Spriggans, and Knockers... be very wary of the Knockers.

On the trek the ocean will remain at your right shoulder, acting as a constant reminder of just where you are. As the evening sky darkens, the sea's vastness will be enhanced by the points of light emanating from the variety of vessels that still use it as a highway, or as a means of scratching a living. The blinking lights will lead your eyes to the horizon, which, in the gloom of dusk, will be just distinguishable as a faint frontier between water and sky. Sometimes, depending on where you are on a particular evening, the horizon will remain unbroken, maybe now and then you'll make out the shadow of a trawler on the dog watch, or a tanker slowly ploughing its way to port in the Solent or the Bay of Biscay.

Sometimes you'll catch the wink of a distant lighthouse; its sweeping beam catching the mist drawn by the cooling air from the sea. Which lighthouse? Well that depends on how far you've got on your journey. If you are just setting off then behind you, across the expanse of St Ives Bay, will be Godrevy lighthouse, perched on its own rock (called Godrevy Island funnily enough) off Godrevy Point. Along the way, heading west, then south-west, then south, you'll get the chance to inspect at close quarters Pendeen Watch, a beautiful building, brilliant white with green trim. Looking down from its cliff-top perch at the tumult below you'll understand just why it was deemed prudent to build it there. Walk a mile or so further along, and a glimpse out to sea may or may not, depending on the weather, reveal a low grey mass on the horizon. Stare for a while and it will become apparent that you're looking at another land, the Scillies or the Isles of Scilly (but never, ever the Scilly Isles). In the summertime the sun sets right behind these mythical lands, silhouetting them against a sky that will pass from an electric blue, through yellow, to indigo, as the day bids its farewell. Stay a while longer and the lighthouses of Pen Enys to

the right and Round Island to the left introduce themselves, winking their warning.

A hike past the engine houses of Botallack and Cape Cornwall (the only cape in Britain) and the sandy reaches of Whitesand Bay up to Pedn-mên-du at the southern end, and the Longships lighthouse will present itself, protecting vessels from catastrophe at Land's End. Head east, across the exposed cliffs towards Porthgwarra, and with another look out across the ocean you may see Wolf Rock, an isolated lighthouse standing 9 miles out to sea. The story of its construction will boggle the mind.

Porthgwarra marks the turning point in the quest; as you head east-north-east you'll encounter the beauty of Porthcurno, with the ancient fortress of Treryn Dinas prominent and unmistakable. Beyond that you're heading for Lamorna, and a glimpse ahead will reveal the coastline of the Lizard peninsula; the lights of Praa Sands, Porthleven and Mullion Cove punctuate the stretch. Beyond the secluded and sandy reaches of Porthcurno sits the last of the lighthouses to be constructed on the peninsula: Tater-du, which was built in 1965. She is a thoroughly modern lighthouse having been automated from the outset. The path beyond its rocky outcrop will soon lead you into the major settlements of the region, beginning with Mousehole, a small and neat traditional fishing village, then on to Newlyn, a slightly less quaint, and certainly more business-like port that still harbours a sizeable fishing fleet. Penzance beyond has all the trappings of a modern provincial town, good and bad, and a hike across the far western end of Mount's Bay will see you arrive at your ultimate goal: St Michael's Mount.

The journey is fascinating, exhausting, but worth the blisters. If this book manages to capture but a modicum of the experience then I think my labours would not have been in vain. Enjoy.

Oliver Hawker, December 2002.

I

AS YOU WERE WALKING IN ST IVES

The name St Ives derives from St Ia, an Irish princess who arrived in Cornwall, apparently on a giant leaf, in the fifth century. She attained martyrdom at the hands of King Theodric of Cornwall, and shortly after her demise the village became known by the name Sancte Ye or Seynt Iysse, which later evolved into its modern form. It was Lelant, however, that dominated the bay until the fourteenth century when its harbour was eventually inundated by the ever-encroaching sands. The import trade Lelant lost as a result was transferred to St Ives and from there the town grew.

Today St Ives has more B&Bs, hotels, restaurants, burger bars and tourists, per square mile than any other town in the region. It is here that many visitors set up base camp and explore the outlying areas of interest. Tourism is now by far the town's biggest money earner. As this is a book concerning the coast path let us concentrate on the points of interest along the coastal fringes of the town.

St Ives town is set on the western side of St Ives Bay. This great expanse of water is fringed by golden beaches, notably the great swathe of sand stretching from Carrack Gladden to Godrevy Point on the eastern seaboard. This far side of the bay is at the full mercy of the elements; Hayle Towans, a great fortress of sand-dunes blown to considerable elevations over the centuries, pays homage to that. The western side of the bay is where the main settlements of the area can be found. These include Hayle, Lelant, Carbis Bay and, to the far west, St Ives. The shallow waters of the bay provided favourable conditions in which fishermen from the villages would cast their nets to catch the huge shoals of pilchards that arrived in the waters during the autumn.

From the bus station a flight of steps will lead you down opposite the Pedn Olva Hotel, which sits on the site of an old copper mine. The road that leads down into the town is aptly named The Warren and is a typical example of the sort of thoroughfare for which St Ives is famed. At the end of the rows of private houses and B&Bs stands a number of artists' studios. Peer through the large windows and it will be possible to see the artists at work. The Warren will eventually bring you out by the war memorial and opposite the church.

St Ives looking from the Porthminster Hotel. Pedn Olva is the headland in the foreground. The harbour area and The Island with the chapel on the summit sit behind.

An odyssey must begin somewhere so this one shall start outside the Porthminster Hotel, a typical Victorian affair perched high above Porthminster Beach commanding spectacular views of the town away to the west. From here it is a short walk down to the railway station that brings many a tourist into the town on a branch line from St Erth. Walking through the car park beyond the station you will come to an area known as the Malakoff, due to its similarity in appearance to a defensive system built around the town of Sebastopol, which was successfully stormed by a joint British and French operation on 8 September 1855 during the Crimean War. A Barbara Hepworth sculpture entitled *Epidaurous* sits amongst the flower beds (more about Barbara later). From the Malakoff, which also doubles as a bus station, you can appreciate the unusual shape of the town as it spreads out below you. The oldest part was built around the harbour area and across the sand bar which connects The Island (also known as St Ives Head) to the mainland.

For many years after trade switched to St Ives the town did not have a church of its own. Lelant held on to its parochial powers which meant that the inhabitants of St Ives had to trek there to bury their dead or baptise their babies. Viewing this as a great hardship in 1408 the people of St Ives petitioned Lord Champeron (Lord of the Manor of St Ives) to intercede with the Pope to licence a chapel. The present parish church was begun in the reign of Henry V and finished in the reign of Henry VI; it took sixteen years to build.

In 1488 a charter was granted to Lord Broke, a later Lord of the Manor, whereby a market could be held every Saturday. The charter also granted permission to hold two annual fairs. A market house was built in 1490 on the site of the present one, which was built in 1832.

On the other side of the market house, on the site the Chinese restaurant now occupies, stood the George and Dragon Inn, the scene of a shocking, albeit amusing, story:

The Act of Uniformity in 1549 enforced the use of a common prayer book written in English. This, however, provoked outrage amongst the people of the county to whom Latin, although still a foreign language, nevertheless represented a safe familiarity in church services. The 1549 Prayer Book Rebellion, as the uprising became known, started in Sampford Courtenay in Devon where parishioners forced their local priest to don his old papist robes and perform Mass. The Cornish soon demanded the same from their priests. During the aftermath of this rebellion one or two inhabitants of St Ives were on the end of some pretty rough treatment by those wanting to punish anybody that dared to revolt in defence of their religious rights. The portreeve at the time, a sort of early mayor, was John Payne and he had taken an active role in the rebellion. Wishing to gain favour with the man charged with suppressing the insurrection in the county, Sir Antony Kingston, he decided to hold a banquet in his honour at the George and Dragon Inn. During the revelries Kingston took Payne to one side and announced that a hanging would have to take place in the town, to show the inhabitants that rebellion could not go unpunished. He instructed that a set of gallows was to be erected immediately and completed before the banquet was over. Payne sent out the orders. On their completion the Provost Marshall duly informed the unsuspecting Payne that the first neck in the noose would be his. A memorial to the hapless portreeve can be seen on the wall of the Catholic church on Tregenna Hill. His coat of arms was also carved on a pew in the parish church.

The alley leading from the church to the sea brings you out on Lambeth Walk. To the right is a large black wooden building, once the studio of Louis Grier, an Australian painter, that played host to the first arts club to be founded in the town in the autumn of 1888. It was not until 1890 that St Ives' Arts Club was officially formed. Its premises were on Westcotts Quay and boasted a membership of some 60 artists. A founding member of the club was Wylie Grier whose works included *A Golden Autumn Eventide* and *Light Lingers on Lowland*.

There is a distinct quality of light in St Ives. Even on overcast days, when the sea appears to be a gun-metal grey, it gives out a luminosity that permeates the town. St Ives is almost surrounded by ocean and the light reflected off it from all angles gives it a Mediterranean sumptuousness, enhanced by the whitewashed buildings in Downalong. So it comes as no surprise to discover the multitude of artists' studios. As well as the light, there is the architecture, the beaches and headlands, and the moors that rise above the town. These provided the attraction to the pioneers of the artists' colony, which has now achieved international recognition with the opening of the Tate Gallery overlooking Porthmeor Beach.

One of the early artists to settle in the town was James Abbott McNeill Whistler who, with two young assistants, Walter Sickert and Mortimer Menpes, arrived in the winter of 1883–84. Whistler was rather a tempestuous fellow, always in the limelight and always controversial. He trained in Paris with Charles Gleyre and became a pupil of Courbet where he studied the doctrine of Realism. Described as being self-absorbed, sophisticated and vain, his quick wit and extraordinary talent soon made him a central figure in Paris and London life. In 1861 he painted in Brittany and it was there that he first became recognised through his work *Alone With The Tide*. His encounter with the ocean

Victorian view of St Ives.

Walk around St Ives at any time of the year and you'll soon come across an artist at work.

soon forced him to repudiate his Realism ideals and he went for the aesthetic 'art for art's sake' approach, endeavouring to 'capture the drama of revealed beauty as seen in a fleeting glimpse at dawn or dusk.' In the 1870s Whistler was based in London, and at the height of his powers. He was in contact with Monet, Degas and a host of other Impressionist painters, but like all good artists he was poor, mainly owing to a lawsuit he filed against John Ruskin. Although he won a farthing in damages it was a hollow victory; his autocratic behaviour in the dock and the public ridicule the case invited, drove his patrons away. In May 1879 he was declared bankrupt. During this period he made a working visit to St Ives to paint seascapes for an exhibition in a Bond Street gallery. On his arrival he was immediately captivated by the town and its light. He had already sent his two assistants ahead to prepare for his arrival, and for three months the party stayed at 14 Barnoon Terrace, overlooking the harbour. Whistler became fascinated by the sea and recorded it in such works as *The Angry Sea*, *Cliffs and Breakers* and *Low Tide*.

St Ives was put on the map as a place of inspiration for artists and soon others arrived, converting old lofts and dilapidated houses into working studios. The arrival of the likes of H. Harewood Robinson, Hon. Duff Tollemache and William Eadie soon saw St Ives begin to rival Newlyn (more of which much later) as a honey-pot for artists. The town was perhaps better equipped to tend to their needs; golf, tennis, bathing, and a darkroom for photographers, were all available at the Porthminster Hotel.

The artists were viewed with an amused curiosity by the people of the town (although on one occasion a Japanese painter was pelted with stones as he set up his easel on the quay – not for being Japanese, but because he was painting on a Sunday). Apart from the odd boisterous late-night soirée, and the St Ivians were no strangers to those, the artists endeavoured to respect the town and its customs in return.

In 1886 Adrian and Marianne Stokes arrived in the town with an already established reputation. Adrian was much influenced by Whistler as a young man, and had sought his advice on how to become a painter a few years earlier. Whistler's advice was not too helpful; 'just paint, anywhere and anything'. Stokes married Austrian painter, Marianne Preindlsberger, in 1884 and the couple moved to Cornwall in 1886 at the invitation of Stanhope Forbes, an eminent Newlyn painter. They lived in Lelant for a time before moving to St Ives and setting up a studio in Virgin Street. In 1890 Adrian Stokes became the first president of the Arts Club and adopted Whistler's comment that 'The first moment is the artists moment' (relating to the artist's requirement for an

Late-Victorian activity on the harbourside, St Ives.

immediate response to nature) as his unofficial motto. Stokes' time in St Ives, like many artists, shifted his style of painting from the 'typically English sentiment' of his earlier works to a more decorative abstract form of landscape. He produced fine seascapes such as *The Harbour Bar* painted in 1883 and *Off St Ives* in 1890; his maturing style is evident in the latter. In 1888 he gained national recognition with his work *Uplands And Sky*, an evening study of the Hayle river. Marianne was predominantly a figure painter. She produced two particularly fine works: *Childhood Wonders*, which depicts three children watching newly born puppies, and *Go, Thou Must Play Alone My Boy, Thy Sister Is In Heaven* painted in 1889. Both artists left St Ives late in the century to set up in London.

The artists' colony of St Ives was very cosmopolitan in the early years. Many of the painters would often move around, switching between St Ives, Paris, Antwerp, Northern France and Scandinavia. Howard Butler, an American artist, wrote in a letter to his father:

There are many artists here, lately there has arrived from Finland a young lady of wonderful talent... We have also in our colony an Austrian, a German, a Norwegian, a Swede, an Irishman, a Scotsman, a Canadian, four Americans and several Englishmen. We had a Greek who we are glad to have gotten rid of!

Butler arrived in St Ives in 1886 and found it:

... more beautiful than any of the French ports. Here the water is pure as crystal, the old town is fully as picturesque as Honfleur, the fishermen are splendid models, the coast is rugged and the sea heavy, colour exceedingly rich. The only drawback, as on the coast of Maine – sea fogs.

He found lodgings away from the hustle and bustle of the harbour and its fishy smells, overlooking Porthmeor Beach, converting an old net loft into a studio. He cut a skylight in the roof and whitewashed the walls. In the space of nine years he was able to report to his father that no less than twenty-four other artists had done the same, in his row of buildings alone.

Another American to spend time in the town was Alexander Harrison. In 1899 he stayed at the Tregenna Castle Hotel. He came with a considerable reputation for painting nudes. His piece *Arcadia*, now hanging in the Louvre in Paris, shows three girls relaxing in an orchard as dappled sunlight falls on them. It is a particularly fine painting, as is *The Wave*, which was considered a tour de force, especially as he painted from memory, remembering how the nocturnal effects of light played on the surface of the sea.

Anders Zorn, a Swedish artist, spent the winter of 1887–88 in St Ives. His best-known work from his visit is *Fishermen, St Ives* which was later purchased by the French Government.

With the onset of the First World War things quietened down in the colony. Painters still worked there but few had the impact of those pioneers, most of whom had left to become academics at various art establishments around the globe. However, a revival took place in the 1920s; St Ives became a centre of the new Modernist movement in painting.

In 1928, two painters, Ben Nicholson and Christopher Wood, were visiting the town for the first time. Having spent a day sightseeing they were on their way back to their lodgings when they happened to peer into an open doorway in Back Road. The home belonged to Alfred Wallis, a retired fisherman. Wallis had gone to sea at the age of nine as a cabin boy and by the age of eighteen was making regular trips from Penzance to the coast of Newfoundland. He got married aged twenty, to Susan Ward, who was twenty-one years his senior and mother to seventeen children. He eventually gave up fishing, having no money for a boat of his own or even a share in one. In 1890 the couple moved to St Ives where Alfred set himself up as a scrap-metal merchant. He was eventually able to save enough money to retire in 1912, when he moved to Back Road. Susan died in 1922 and Wallis became a somewhat lonely figure.

It was at this point that he started to paint, and it was this work that the two young artists saw as they peered in through the door that afternoon. Early-twentieth-century artists had tired of the pretty romanticism of the Impressionists and were searching for a fresh vision that would add a vitality to their work; the innocent eye of a child. In Wallis' paintings Nicholson saw a clear sense of design, an unpretentious creative energy, a childlike simplicity and a verification of the direction towards which he was already travelling. Wallis' sense of perspective followed his own system and he painted objects that were most important to him: Smeaton's Pier, the lighthouse, the harbour. His boats he painted with great care and attention, the detail of the rigging and sails all from memory of the vessels he worked on as a younger man. He used boat paint on scraps of card, or household objects, anything he could get his hands on.

Nicholson's own works *St Ives Bay, Sea with Boats* (1931) and *Porthmeor Beach* (1929) clearly show the influence Wallis had on him. In 1939 he moved to St Ives with his second wife, sculptor Barbara Hepworth, and helped inspire a renaissance in the town.

Alfred Wallis c.1890.

'The Sailing Ship', a painting by Alfred Wallis.

The torch of exciting, challenging and sometimes bewildering Modernist art has been carried through to modern times in St Ives by the likes of Peter Lanyon, Terry Frost and Patrick Heron. Fine examples of their work can be seen in the splendid Tate Gallery which is a work of art in its own right.

Meanwhile back in the distant past... In 1639 St Ives became a municipality. A mayoral seat was established along with a recorder, a town clerk and a Corporation of a dozen aldermen and two dozen burgesses. The last portreeve, Thomas Stevens, was replaced by the first mayor, Richard Hext. Francis Basset commemorated the event by donating a loving cup inscribed with the words:

If any discord twixt my friends arise
Within the borough of St Ives
It is desired that this my cup of Love
To Evrie one a peace maker may prove
Then am I blessed to have given a legacy
So like my heart unto prosperity.

In the seventeenth century, St Ives came under the increasing influence of the Puritans, and as a result became one of only two boroughs in Cornwall sympathetic to the Parliamentary cause. In 1644 Puritans from St Ives, Zennor and Towednack assembled on Longstone Down. This spurred Sir Richard Grenville, leader of the Royalists in Cornwall, into action. He summoned a force to head off the threat. Outnumbered, the Parliamentarians fled the scene. The Royalists entered St Ives and fined Mayor Hammond £500 for not controlling the populace. He refused to pay and was imprisoned at Launceston, but was later released on the orders of Charles I.

While Grenville was in St Ives he arranged the hanging of a Zennor man, and later two St Ives men were sent to the gallows in Truro. The leader of the Parliamentary forces, Sir John Arundell, escaped capture and later went to fight alongside Fairfax, receiving the Royalist surrender at Truro in 1646. The people of St Ives fared a little better when a Colonel Gorig tried to enter the town, only to find all routes into the town blocked by pilchard barrels filled with sand. He was forced to retire to Penzance.

The year 1647 saw St Ives gripped with plague. Half the people fled the town and farmers were afraid to enter, instead leaving their harvests by the streams at Polmanter Water (near Halsetown) and Carbis Bay. The townsfolk left their payment in the streams to be collected after they were safely out of harm's way.

The continued food shortage soon brought the town to near-famine but at the critical point a ship belonging to a Mr Opye from Plymouth entered the harbour. The Corporation purchased its entire cargo for £196, distributed the wheat for free, and sold the wine for 12d. a quart. St Ives was saved.

From the Arts Club the railed walkway continues to the harbour area, the focal point of the town. The first point of interest is the lifeboat station situated at the top of the slip. The earliest recorded shipwreck in the waters around St Ives occurred on the day of the execution of Charles I. The *Garland*, carrying the King's personal effects, was wrecked off Godrevy Island with the loss of 60 lives. A man and a boy were the only survivors, living on seaweed and rainwater for two days before being plucked off the island. This event was only one of many that eventually led to the building of the lighthouse on the island in 1859.

St Ives was home to several pilots and salvagers known as 'hobblers' who supplemented their income from fishing by guiding ships safely into harbour. These men also put their own lives at risk whenever a ship got into trouble.

The establishment of a full-time, purpose-built lifeboat in St Ives came about as a result of a competition. Mr Francis Jennings Adams won the contest set up by the Royal Polytechnic Society to design a model lifeboat, the design of which went on to be used for the real thing. The 30ft *Hope* was kept in a shed 400yds above the high-water mark in the charge of local fisherman Mr Hockin. In 1861 a branch of the RNLI was set up and a new boat-house was built for the new lifeboat, the self-righting *Moses*. This boat saw its first real action the following winter when the French brig *Providence* capsized twice. The Emperor of France awarded the coxswain a gold medal for the service.

In 1866 the *Moses* was replaced by a bigger boat. A larger boat-house was also built to allow for launching onto Fore Strands. Despite the superstition that says it is bad luck to rename a boat, the *Moses* was renamed the *Exeter*. She saw action in December 1867 when a violent storm, severe enough to damage the newly constructed pier, forced the French coal carrier *Courier du Nord* onto a sand ridge outside Smeaton's Pier. Despite help from the *Exeter*, the *Nord* eventually drifted onto Porthminster Beach.

In 1886 a 34ft lifeboat was built, also named *Exeter*. She was away on exercises, however, when a violent storm forced the steamers *Bessie*, *Vulture* and *Gintra* onshore at Carbis Bay. The reserve lifeboat was called but, because of the heavy seas, it was unable to clear St Ives harbour. It was left to the inshore team to rescue the crew of the steamers.

The modern harbour at low tide.

One of the longest-serving St Ives lifeboats, the *James Stevens* began service in 1900. She attended distress calls for 33 years. In January 1908, she battled to save the *Lizzie R. Wilce*, out of Falmouth, that was stuck on rocks off Porthminster Beach. The war years saw plenty of action for the lifeboat. In 1915 she was involved in a co-ordinated rescue with the *Helen Peele* lifeboat from Padstow, of the SS *Taunton* of Liverpool. The vast majority of rescues attempted during this period were of torpedoed ships, hit in the Bristol Channel.

A new lifeboat station opened to house the state-of-the-art *Caroline Oats & William Maine* in June 1940. She was launched by a tractor across the harbour sands and saw much service, coming to the aid of ditched aircraft, both British and German, and many naval casualties.

After the Second World War tourism took hold in St Ives and consequently the lifeboat was called to assist stricken holiday-makers, caught unawares by the swift tidal currents. The Oakley-class lifeboat *Frank Penfold Marshall* arrived in July 1969 and served for twenty years. For most of that period its coxswain was Thomas Cocking, who became one of the most decorated such men in lifeboat history. An example of his selfless fortitude came when he jumped overboard from a motor launch and swam to rescue a young boy clinging to rocks off St Ives Head. The lifeboat was involved in a well-known co-ordinated rescue in August 1979, when the search was on for survivors of the Fastnet Race, hit by a gale and heavy seas. For nine hours a total of eight lifeboats, a Nimrod aircraft and HMS *Anglesey*, searched the seas for signs of life. The *Frank Penfold Marshall* saw her last major rescue in 1989. She, along with the reserve lifeboat, stood by to assist a winching operation involving a helicopter from RNAS *Culdrose*. In storm-force winds sixteen crew members were hauled to safety when their ship, the *Secil Japan*, hit rocks at Deadman's Cove. The lifeboats searched in vain for one man who lifted his arms too soon to get into the helicopter and slipped through the winch strop.

The new lifeboat station was built on its present site in 1990. The lifeboat it now houses is named *The Princess Royal*. She is a Mersey-class boat, about 39ft in length. Her two engines are each capable of producing 285hp, allowing the boat to reach 17.5 knots, with a range of about 180 miles.

In all the years a full-time lifeboat has been operating in St Ives, over 1000 lives have been saved, and many more assisted to safety.

The harbour in St Ives represented the chief port of departure to Ireland in the sixteenth century. Several entries in the borough records of the time relate to this traffic, and record the generosity of the town to unfortunate travellers.

For example, 'The sum of one schilling paid to a man of Irelande that had his bark stolen by Pirats'.

No contemporary account exists describing to the look of the harbour at this time but it is known that prior to 1766 the pier ran out from Porth Glaze. It was probably made of timber filled with rubble but the maintenance and the need to keep the area clear of sand (a recurring problem in this region) were constant drains on the public coffers.

In 1766 a new stone pier, designed by John Smeaton, was commissioned. It was built out from the Castle Rocks, and at the same time the old pier was dismantled and the wharf built. The pier was only half its present length but sheltered a greater expanse of water and prevented sand creeping into the harbour. The result was a vast increase in traffic which was reflected in the harbour dues. These totalled only £593 in 1770 but reached £1824 in 1836. This revenue was lost when the town was declared a free port in 1837.

In 1847 a total of 735 men were employed in the pilchard industry, working some 400 boats. Around 100 men were engaged in other types of fishing and countless others were involved in industries dependent on fishing. The hustle and bustle of the place meant that boats jockeyed for anchorage and on more than one occasion fishermen came to blows on account of this. A new harbour was constructed on the seaward side of Smeaton's Pier at right angles to it, but its exposed position meant that after only twenty years' use it was reduced to a wreck by the constant pounding from the waves.

In 1886 the petty disputes erupted into a full-blown riot as the fishermen vented their anger at the authorities whom they saw as doing little to alleviate the problem of overcrowding. The rioters were placated by the lengthening of Smeaton's Pier in 1888. A shorter pier was built on the western side of the harbour in 1894. This served as a loading jetty for the road stone quarried from the Carthew and Orange Lane sites nearby. In 1922 the wharf road was extended from the lifeboat station to Chy-an-Chy to provide relief for Fore Street.

St Ives town was traditionally divided into two halves; Downalong and Upalong. The boundaries that separated the two are not so clear today, but the main part of Downalong occupied the sand bank connecting the harbour with what once was The Island, on which the chapel now sits. This area is a rabbit warren of narrow streets. Traditional fishing cottages stand huddled as if holding each other up. In a thoroughfare called the Digey stands an arch; this is all that is left of the Hicks family mansion, but the courtyard still remains and is called Hicks Court.

The extended Smeaton's Pier with its modern lighthouse. The old lighthouse marks the end of the pier prior to the extension.

In Victoria Road there is a house built on a rock that was once a pub called the Labour in Vain. The pub sign depicted a washerwoman scrubbing a black boy, reputedly the sole survivor of a ship grounded at Porthmeor. The woman took the boy into her care and immediately set about trying to scrub him 'clean.'

On the north end of Smeaton's Pier stands the Chapel of St Leonard which once served as a place of worship and contemplation for fishermen. A friar was in residence and would say prayers before the fishermen went to sea, receiving in payment fish and wine. It is known to have occupied the site before Smeaton's Pier was built because it served as a blacksmith shop during the development.

From the chapel a right turn onto the rocks below the old wooden pier will allow walkers, at low tide, to rejoin the path below the imposing walls of the old castle. Lord Broke, he of the 1488 charter, was responsible for the castle, the site of which had always been utilised for defensive purposes against invaders from the sea. Coastal towns such as St Ives were often the first line of defence.

St Ia Church in St Ives still dominates the skyline of the town.

Looking across Porthmeor from the Chapel of St Nicholas.

The Chapel of St Nicholas on The Island.

The Tate Gallery.

As the town matured into a thriving commercial centre, improved organisation at local-government level allowed St Ives to prosper. During the reign of Queen Mary II (1689–94) the town had the dubious fortune of being able to submit two members to the House of Commons. This gave it the distinction of being one of the most notorious rotten boroughs in the country. This fact was not lost on many an opportunistic would-be MP wishing to gain an easy (though expensive in terms of bribes) entry to parliament.

Two frequent visitors to Cornwall in the seventeenth century were John and Charles Wesley, founders of the Methodist movement. The initial truculence of the Cornish to these religious revolutionaries is well documented. A St Ives woman wrote in her journal, during their first visit on 30 August 1743: 'Charles Wesley is come to town, to try, if he can, to pull the churches down'.

A second visit the following month ended in John getting a smack in the mouth after one of his sermons was interrupted by a mob. A year later, when he was leaving the house of a friend, John Nance, he was pelted with stones. The established churches were alarmed by the Wesleys and did all they could to demonise them and their message. After a local vicar had given a sermon in

The old castle walls.

which he affiliated Methodist teaching with papists and Jacobites, two rather rampant bees in the bonnets of the population of the time, riots broke out in the town, forcing the mayor to literally read the Riot Act. However, by 1745 the Cornish had warmed to the message and eventually the Methodists acquired a strong foothold in the county.

Porthgwidden car park now occupies what would have been the site of the castle itself. Below the car park the small beach that is Porthgwidden is a popular choice for families because of the row of beach huts to the rear. From the beach the path then takes you onto The Island. The chapel on the summit of The Island is dedicated to St Nicholas. Away to the right is the National Coastwatch Institute's lookout station. Called Lamprock, because of the pharos light that used to occupy the site, the station is manned during daylight hours.

Porthmeor Beach stretches long and wide all the way from The Island to Carrick Du. It is a great surfing beach where suitable conditions for the sport prevail for most of the year. The road that follows the low cliff at the back of the beach is home to the Tate Gallery. At the foot of Porthmeor Hill stands the ancient holy well of Venton Eia or St Ia's Well. The well served as one of the few freshwater supplies for the townspeople, and in 1693 it was covered, faced and floored with hewn granite rocks, which is how it remains today.

Along from the well the coast path begins. As you skirt the western edge of Porthmeor Beach, the path is a comfy tarmac, and undulates gently over the soft contours leading up to Carrick Du. Many people are fooled into thinking that this stretch, akin to a leisurely stroll in the park, is what the rest of the journey is like. But any illusions they may have had are soon dispelled as they round the first headland and are greeted with the sight of rugged cove, punctuated with rugged headland, intermixed with rugged cliff top. So make the most of this gentle introduction to your quest, because you will soon be out in the wilds.

Note: The author is indebted to Tom Cross for his history of the artists of Newlyn and St Ives which appear in the trilogy *The Shining Sands, Painting the Warmth of the Sun,* and *Catching the Wave* (Halsgrove).

2

NO REST TILL THE TINNERS

Those that have walked the South West Coast Path will tell you that the trek from St Ives to the next port of call, Zennor, is very hard going. I used to work the bar at the Tinners Arms in Zennor, one place that is a definite watering hole along the way, and during the summer months at around 1.30pm the rush would begin. Hot and thirsty souls would stagger to the bar and point in a rather delirious manner at the sign that said 'Cream teas available here', throw their money down and collapse in a heap. After they had recovered their senses I was able to ascertain that they had set off from St Ives at around ten o'clock that morning to walk the path to Zennor. In roughly three-and-a-half hours – and these people weren't spring chickens – they had covered about 6 miles of

The rock-strewn Burthallan cliffs.

On the way to Clodgy Point.

the toughest terrain the path had to offer in this neck of the woods. On a blistering hot day they were fit for nothing else by lunch-time! Most waited for one of the two buses that passed during the day to carry them back to St Ives where they probably snoozed away the rest of the afternoon or tended their oozing blisters. You have been warned!

The path begins proper at the far side of Porthmeor Beach, and it is not long before St Ives is out of sight and you are heading for Carrick Du. It rises to cross the top of some low cliffs before reaching Clodgy Point. The Burthallan cliffs above Clodgy Point are made up of pillow lavas, formed when erupting lava oozed from the seabed and rolled down the local slope before coming to rest and moulding itself into depressions formed by earlier eruptions.

If there has been a particularly dry spell prior to your journey then you may be able to keep to the cliff edges throughout this stretch. But, as is usually the case, one or two detours inland may be required due to the boggy conditions brought about by water pouring from the many springs in the area. The National Trust purchased this stretch of coast in 1957 when St Ives Council proposed plans to turn the area into a rubbish dump. Can you imagine?

Inland rise the summits of Trevalgan and Rosewall Hills, which are intersected by the main coast road. On Trevalgan Hill a plaque has been placed in memory of the artist Peter Lanyon, a prominent figure in the St Ives school, who died in a gliding accident in 1964.

The headland that lies between Clodgy and Hor Points has on it the remnants of a cottage that probably belonged to a tin prospector or farmer. You will come across many of these abandoned ruins on your journey. The path joins a farm track and goes across Hellesveor Cliff. A right turn will take you down to Hor Point. Here are the remains of a small copper working, next to which is a huge shaft. The workings were run by a Captain Martin Dunn, who built the engine house. To the left of the shaft is a circular platform, with a diameter of about 35ft, which may have been a horse-driven whim. Great caution is advised in these areas of old mine workings.

The path rises from Hor Point and crosses the Trowan Cliffs, which stand high above a very attractive cove between Hor and Pen Enys Points.

Pen Enys Point was purchased by the National Trust in 1984. As with most of their purchases along the coastline, the landscape has been transformed from agriculture to more wildlife-friendly habitats.

Peregrine falcons can once more be seen hovering high, then shooting down at breathtaking velocities to catch their prey which hides amongst the regener-ated heathland. In built-up areas pigeons are the mainstay of this impressive

Approaching Pen Enys.

raptor's diet. On the coast, voles, stoats and rabbit kittens, along with smaller birds, make up the bulk of its diet. The highest recorded attack velocity measured almost 175mph. Nests are usually found in wooded or rocky areas, and are sometimes converted from nests vacated by other raptors. Three to four eggs are usually laid and incubated for the most part by the hen. At 35 to 40 days the chicks are ready to leave the nest, but stay close by for a while longer before being encouraged to leave by the parents.

The area around the headland forms part of an inland trail set up by the owners of Trevalgan Farm. They have set out a route marked by information boards. Trevalgan Cliff towers over the coves of Polgassick and Brea, and it is between the two that the cargo steamer *Bessemer City* came to grief on 2 November 1936. Her cargo of tinned food emptied into the sea to be salvaged, minus their labels, by the locals. Meal times were a constant source of suspense for weeks afterwards. It is also at this point in 1950 that 20 cows fell over the cliff. Most were eventually rescued by the police and coastguards using hoists, but one or two sadly drowned. They say that the sea bass that was caught here the following season was the biggest for years.

The next headland is Carn Naun Point. Here at the Ordinance Survey triangulation point you can catch breathtaking views in all directions. Inland, the peaks of Rosewall Hill, Trendrine Hill, and Zennor Hill are before you. Leading away to the west are Hannibals Carn, Carn Galver and Watch Croft, with Pendeen Carn in the far distance. On the coast Zennor Head, Gurnard's Head and Pendeen Watch give you some idea of just how far you have yet to go. Out to sea lie The Carracks (ahead), Godrevy Island (behind you on the far side of St Ives Bay), and Trevose Head (way off to the east).

On from Carn Naun you soon approach River Cove, and it is here that a little sojourn inland is worth the effort. The tiny and now abandoned settlement of Treveal was home to a community of 70 people in the late-nineteenth century. Most of the land in this area was owned by the Bristol shipping firm, the Haine Estate. It built the farm buildings in the settlement, some of which date from 1882. The river valley leading to Treveal is sheltered from the fierce south-westerly gales, and as a result trees have been able to gain a foothold. This will be a regular theme along the path. One moment you can be walking high on a barren (though not featureless) cliff top before descending into a little oasis of wooded beauty, easily matching anything found in the Cotswolds. The Treveal valley nurtures blackthorn, hawthorn, ash, elder and sycamore trees, as well as a wealth of shrubs and delicate flowers in season.

Carn Naun seen from The Carracks.

The Carracks.

Opposite: *Looking across Porthzennor from Zennor Head.*

Inland a little further from Treveal is Wicca Farm. The farmhouse here was built around 1600 and was the largest dwelling in the Zennor region for 120 years. The earliest farmers settled around Wicca about 3500 years ago, and many of the boundary hedges date back to that time.

Back out on the coast, to the west of Carn Naun lie The Carracks. From St Ives you can catch a boat ride out to Seal Island. At low tide it is possible to scramble down the rocks to sea level. This area of the coast, as the alternative name for The Carracks suggests, is a good place to spot seals. You will probably hear them first as their coats make them very difficult to distinguish from the rock. Most probably you will see grey seals; they are more in evidence than the common seal due to an epidemic of the phocine distemper virus in 1988, that wiped out 10 000 of them. Small numbers of the common seal have begun to make a reappearance along the Channel coast, but sightings this far west are extremely rare indeed.

Grey seals belong to a group of mammals known as pinnipeds. The common ancestor of all the seal species was thought to be a giant otter-like creature that lived some 27 million years ago. Around 2.5 million years ago the

ancestors of the grey seal divided genetically from the phocid seals, which include the common seal. The greys are the largest land-breeding mammals on the British Isles; the males can grow to almost 10ft in length and weigh up to 48 stone. The total population of grey seals around the UK has been estimated at about 108 500, which represents one half of the total world population. Cornwall represents the southernmost limit of the grey seals' territory in the East Atlantic. Grey seal pups are born between late July and October, so you may even be lucky enough to see some, although it is worth noting that their silver coats often mean they are mistaken for common seals. It is also worth noting that bottling, snoozing whilst upright in the water, is the most common way grey seals rest, and the best place to see them at it is Porth Ledden on the eastern side of Cape Cornwall.

Zennor Head looking to Gurnard's Head.

From the rocks around The Carracks it is a steady climb to the headland above Mussel Point. From here you are treated to fantastic views across Wicca Pool to Carn Porth, and Zennor Head beyond. In the bay, at low tide, the Gala Rocks are exposed. The granite in this area has been naturally split along particularly clean fractures, and it was from here that the blocks were cut to build the church at St Ives.

Wicca Pool is a great place to come in late autumn to catch a glimpse of migrating sea birds. Manx Shearwaters have been spotted here on a number of occasions.

From Wicca Pool you cross Tregerthen Cliff, also under the stewardship of the National Trust, and approach Zennor Head. In the lee of this headland is Porthzennor Cove; it is here that a distinctive line appears in the rock strata, as the granite gives way to the killas (a Cornish term meaning the greenstone created during the formation of the region, some 400 million years ago). Zennor Head is so shaped because it is composed of these ancient sedimentary rocks.

Most intrepid coast-path walkers have, by now, nothing else on their minds than a rest, a pint and a pasty. A left turn at Zennor Head will get you onto, heaven forbid, a 'proper' road, which leads you into the first taste of civilisation since you said goodbye to the Tate.

Rest up, and fill your face. There's a long way to go.

3

BEWARE OF THE MERMAID

The first human habitation here has been dated to around 2000–1500BC. The old name for the settlement is Treveglos – the 'farming settlement by the church'. The farm on the left as you approach the village still holds the name. In fields across to the right, were once mills powered by the small stream that runs down and over the precipitous cliffs at the shore.

The church dominates the village of Zennor. It was built in the twelfth century, although the aisle was added in the fifteenth and a comprehensive restoration job was completed in 1890. St Senara is the patron saint of the church; she is apparently linked to Princess Asenora of Brittany who was married to King Geollo. Legend has it that her stepmother was jealous of her beauty and virtue and sought to get rid of her. She did this by falsely accusing her of adultery, for which the punishment was death by burning at the stake. While under arrest, her jailers learned that she was pregnant and so, not wanting to be guilty of murdering the unborn, nailed the Princess into a barrel and threw her into the sea. The barrel drifted for some weeks and its occupant was kept alive by being fed by an angel. She gave birth to the child while still entombed, but eventually the barrel was washed up on the coast of Ireland. The two were recalled to Brittany by a remorseful Geollo , who realised his wife had never been unfaithful. En route they landed in Cornwall and founded the parishes of Zennor and St Budoc. The boy later became abbot, and later patron saint, of St Budoc (meaning 'drowned one').

Zennor and its inhabitants have been the subject of many legends over the years, probably due to the village's utter isolation even by West Penwith's standards. Many of the villagers were once considered to be of 'mean parsimony' due to their poverty. It was said that by their thrifty habits they lived like goats!

Along the walk you will come across many tales of fairies and spirits, so it is best to sort out which is which early on to avoid confusion. First of all you've got the 'Little People' who are the spirits of the Cornish who lived before the time of Christ. These wraiths are gradually getting smaller and smaller – it is

The village of Zennor.

Zennor, seen from Zennor Hill.

not certain whether or not they have actually turned into muryans (ants) yet, but they will eventually. Then there are the Spriggans, descendants of the Trolls of Scandinavia, who dwell in cairns and cromlechs. They have sole charge of all buried treasures so take care if you find any, for they are devious little beggars and likely to do you a mischief. The Piskeys are even more loathsome, but not often seen as they are very unsociable. They cannot hurt you if you turn your coat inside out, so be prepared. The Knockers and Nuggies of the mines will be dealt with later on, so finally we come to the Brownies. These, as their name suggests, are kindly and good household fairies, although sadly they are close to extinction – probably because to survive in the cutthroat world of fairy-land you need to rattle a few cages now and then, and the Brownies just don't have it in them!

There is one particular fairy legend associated with Zennor. There was once a thrifty housewife who lived between Zennor and St Ives. She kept her house spotlessly clean and wasted nothing. One morning during her daily ritual of scrubbing and polishing, there was a knock at the door. She opened it to find a very refined-looking gentlemen. He explained that he had been observing her for some time and admired the way she kept her home in such order. He said that he had in his possession an orphaned baby, and as she had no children of her own could she take care of him, for he knew the infant would come to no harm in such a clean home. She was taken aback a little when the stranger explained that she would have to be blindfolded as she accompanied him back to his house to fetch the babe. However maternal instincts overwhelmed any doubts she had, so she agreed.

The man led her out of her house and she soon felt the land beneath her feet rise sharply. She guessed that she was being led to the summit of Zennor Hill and beyond. They presently reached the man's house, and her blindfold was removed; she was inside a grand mansion. She could only have walked a few miles and, although she had lived in the area all her life, she knew of no houses of this size in the vicinity. Still her desire for a child blinded her to any misgivings. A bell was rung and out trooped a band of servants, carrying the baby boy. He was the most beautiful thing she had ever seen but her custody of him came with conditions. She should never teach him the Lord's Prayer, never wash him after sunset and when she did wash him she was only to use the water left in a white ewer outside her back door every morning. She must never use the water for her own ablutions. For this she would be well rewarded, food would be provided; both her and the boy would want for nothing. Blindfolded once more she was led back to her home near Zennor.

The boy grew up strong and happy. The lady followed the instructions faithfully, and spent many a happy hour watching her charge from the parlour window, playing in the sunshine as if he had company. The years passed and the woman grew older; her skin became wrinkled, and she longed for the complexion of her younger days. It occurred to her that the water from the ewer had given the boy a perfect complexion. Although she knew it was wrong, she washed her face in this water. Afterwards she returned to the parlour to examine her face in the mirror, but as she passed the window she saw that the boy was no longer playing with imaginary companions; indeed he did *have* company. Her garden was swarming with Little People, playing tag with the boy. She realised that the water had enabled her to see into the world of the fairies. Frightened, she ran all the way to her sisters in St Ives, where she bumped into the strange man who had delivered the boy to her. He gave her an enraged look, and with his index finger poked her so hard in the eye that it pushed her eyeball deep into her skull. He screamed at her in fury:

The Zennor mermaid.

The font in Zennor church.

Water for Elf, Not for self
You've lost your eye, your child
And yourself.

Terrified, the old woman staggered home and, with her remaining eye, saw that the boy was gone. She died not long afterwards, some say of hunger, most say of a broken heart.

The legend of the Zennor mermaid is probably one of the best known in this area. Go into the church at Zennor and on the end of a pew you will find a carving of this mermaid, with a comb in one hand and a mirror in the other.

When strangers appear in villages like Zennor they do not go unnoticed, particularly when such strangers are young, female and beautiful. She had started to appear every Sunday at the church for morning service and afterwards walked the path behind the inn back to the cliffs. The locals decided that she was from a nearby village and had resolved to adopt Zennor church as her place of worship, taking the coast path home. Mathey Trewella was smitten, however, and decided one Sunday to follow the mysterious lovely down the path. Suffice to say, he never returned.

Years later a ship was anchored, unusually, off Pendour Cove. Its captain was making repairs to the deck when he heard singing. He looked over the side, straight into the eyes of a mermaid. 'Would you care to remove your anchor' said she, 'for it is blocking the doorway to our home.' She explained that she was eager to get back to her children and husband. After regaining his composure the captain did as the mermaid asked. He then went ashore and told the villagers his story.

The villagers themselves were often the subject of gossip and speculation. At one point it was believed that they had the power to stem the flow of blood. The Zennor Charmers, as they were known, could place their hands over a wound and with the incantation the injury would heal:

Baptised in the Jordan.
The river stood.
So shall thy blood [name of subject].
In the name of the father, son and holy ghost.
Amen.

The one fact about the inhabitants of Zennor that is beyond doubt is that life for them was tough. In their secluded location, without the luxury of a nearby anchorage from where supplies could be delivered, many essential items had to be found from close at hand. For centuries the only sources of fuel were turf, furze (gorse) and sometimes ushen and claws (dry cow's dung).

All the members of the parish had the right to cut fuel and plots were allotted to individual households by the farmers whose lands the cutting site fell within. The cutting areas for Zennor were mainly on Sperris Moor, with the cutting season usually in early May, before the first hay was cut. Biddicks, specialised spades, were used to cut a turf 18in. square and 4in. thick. The slabs were then stood up in pairs, black side out, and left to dry for a couple of weeks before being built into 'pooks'. These were mounds of turf, built up in decreasing circles, filled with further slabs in the middle and topped with an oversized piece. The furze-cutting season was also at the beginning of May. Once the furze had been cut, it was bundled into 'faggots' before being piled into ricks and left to dry until September.

In the 1920s coal replaced these traditional fuels, when it became viable to import it from the pits of South Wales. A horse and cart would go from Zennor to St Ives where it would be weighed on a weighbridge that stood outside the Sloop Inn. It was then driven to Smeaton's Pier where the coal was loaded up. It was weighed again at the weighbridge where the appropriate payment was made before returning to Zennor.

There are many traditions up and down the country that are linked to the annual harvest. Zennor and the surrounding areas have their own, called 'Crying the Neck'. The neck was the name given to the last sheaf of wheat cut in the field. It was held aloft by its reaper, who would then cry 'I have a...! I have a...!' The rest of the workers would then shout in reply 'what ave ee?' to which the reply would come 'A neck, a neck, a neck!' Great celebration and general revelry would then ensue into the early hours. The neck would later be made into a small sheaf, decorated and hung up in the farmhouse kitchen until the next harvest. The spirit of the corn lies within the last neck, and following this tradition would ensure a plentiful harvest the following year.

Many people find the walk from St Ives to Zennor enough for one day. The backpackers' hostel is ideal for an overnight stop; it provides comfortable accommodation plus food. If you fancy a glass of something alcoholic then the Tinners Arms next door is the only place to go. This is a great little pub with plenty of character and very good food.

Next to the hostel you will find the Wayside Museum is an excellent place to delve a little deeper into the history of the Zennor area. It covers all aspects of life in the village from 3000BC to the present. The gift shop is well stocked with

The backpackers' hostel, formerly the Wesleyan chapel.

books on mining, the occult and general history, as well as fine-art pieces, postcards and delicious ice-creams.

The museum was founded by Frederick Christian Hirst (1874–1938). After serving in the military in India, Hirst returned to Zennor in 1924. He scoured the surrounding landscape for prehistoric relics, and had soon amassed a sizeable collection of hand axes, quern stones and other implements. He soon attracted the attention of an American archaeologist, Hugh O'Neill, who invited Hirst to accompany him on an excavation of the Romano-British village at Chysauster. Soon afterwards O'Neill produced the book *The Archaeology Of Cornwall*, since considered to be a landmark publication which helped to seal Cornwall's reputation as one of the richest sources of prehistoric archaeological remains in the world.

The Wayside Museum.

D.H. Lawrence and his wife, Freda, stayed in the village for a short time during the First World War; they rented a cottage at Higher Tregerthen. However, things did not go very well – Freda was German and locals believed her to be a spy. Dismayed at the hostility towards them, the Lawrences soon departed. In his short story, *Kangaroo,* Lawrence launched a thinly-veiled attack on the paranoia and small-mindedness of some people during times of national crisis.

If you fancy hanging around the village for a while, there are plenty of inland walks to be had. One of the most tempting will surely be a hike up Zennor Hill. The path leading to its summit begins on the other side of the main road. It is heavy going but the views are breathtaking.

Zennor Quoit, found at the eastern end of the ridge, was saved from demolition in 1930 by the local vicar who paid a farmer 30s. to prevent him dismantling it and using the slabs to build a pigsty.

4

LOOKS A BIT LIKE A GURNARD

From Zennor you will need to retrace your steps a little in order to rejoin the coast path heading westward. A left turn leads you to a steep descent into Pendour Cove. A stream, the source of which can be found high in the hills beyond Zennor Quoit, flows down the valley and cascades quite beautifully over the cliff edge. A small wooded bridge crosses the stream and the path carries on across Carnelloe Cliff above Veor Cove. There was some mining activity in this area, mainly for copper, and a few buildings remain; although they are well hidden in the undergrowth, there are shafts dotted about, so stay close to the path.

Crossing high above Porthglaze Cove the trail leads to the National Trust-owned Boswednack Cliff. This area is of special biological interest due to its poorly drained rough grazing grounds which support a diversity of 'mire' communities, including St John's Wort, southern marsh orchid, bog pimpernel and royal fern. Here also is a good example of a prehistoric terraced field system, thought to date from the late Iron Age.

On the western flanks of Boswednack Cliff there are great views westward across Lean Point and Treen Cove to the old fortress of Gurnard's Head. Lean Point played host to an old pilchard factory in the nineteenth century. Here the pilchards were packed into hogsheads and loaded for shipment to Mediterranean destinations.

From the old pilchard works the path crosses a private road (which, incidentally, leads to a spectacularly situated B&B) and brings you out on the neck of Gurnard's Head. This headland is one of the most striking promontories on the route. It is so named because of its similarity in appearance to the gurnard fish. The Cornish name for the headland is Trereen Dinas, meaning 'castle on the high place', a name which is echoed in the similar-looking promontory near Porthcurno, Treryn Dinas.

Evidence of the headland's ancient use as a defensive fort is still just about visible. Three weather-worn stone ramparts stretch across the narrowest part of the neck at the far end, and a total of 16 house platforms have been identified

The sun hits the peak of Gurnard's Head.

Gurnard's Head, looking across Treen Cove.

Looking down to Porthmeor Cove from Carn Galver.

on the eastern slopes. These features date back to the second century BC, and terraced field systems have also been discovered adjacent to the footpath leading to the hamlet of Treen. These were probably in use when the fortress was occupied.

The remains of an engine house stands on the neck. This is the first opportunity to inspect such a building at close quarters on the walk (but it certainly won't be your last). The building once housed a 30in. pumping or beam engine. Its job was to keep the water out of the two adjacent mine shafts.

The mine at Gurnard's Head began life as the Treen Copper Mine some time before 1821, and its first shaft was sunk on a small rocky outcrop near the water's edge (possibly Lean Point). A 10ft wall was required to keep the sea out of the shaft during high spring tides. In 1837 the mine became called Gurnard's Head Mine, and the shaft was deepened to 250ft below sea level. At this time water-power was still being used to pump the ever-flooding shaft, but in 1843 a new company took over the mine and built the engine house in evidence today. Despite some good finds of copper the site was shut down in 1847, and never used again.

There are a number of routes you can take to get to the end of Gurnard's Head. The high path will lead right across its spine, whereas the low path crosses the sheltered eastern meadows and is close to the cliff edge. Once inside this ancient fortress you will appreciate the shelter it provides from the howling winds. The sound of the roaring ocean is also blocked out, so a moment of calm and utter solitude can be had before heading westward again. In more recent times the very tip of the headland hosted a small coastguard lookout, and huers used the site to spot shoals of pilchards. More of them later.

From the headland the path crosses Treen Cliff, over Carn Gloose and continues towards Porthmeor Point, another NT-managed area. This region is at the heart of an ancient farming landscape. The farms here took (and still take) advantage of the wide variation in topograghy; rough grazing on the moorland, cultivation of the fertile soil across the wave-cut plateau and further grazing and furze cutting on the cliff tops.

On entering Porthmeor Cove you get the chance to appreciate the way the land rises dramatically from sea level, all the way to the summit of Carn Galver. The cove itself plays host to some unusual geological features; on the far side near sea level the granite has intruded into the older sedimentary rock, leaving spidery veins that lead up the cliff side.

A small, ancient-looking stone bridge crosses this valley's well-utilised stream and from then on the path leaves you to your own devices, for it disintegrates into a mire of cattle-trodden land that covers the slope leading up to the Carn Moyle Cliff. Things don't get any clearer once up high again, but if you pick your way carefully across Carn Veslan Cliff ahead, you will be met with the impressive sight of the boulder-strewn northern slope of Bosigran Castle, home of Ygrain, mother of King Arthur.

Now, there are those who will try to fob you off with fairy tales that the name Bosigran derives from the old Cornish for 'dwelling place of the Crane' or 'dwelling place in the dry valley'. This is of course nonsense. The truth is obvious: Ygrain had turned her back on baby Arthur for just a minute when he fell over the cliff edge and into the sea. He was saved from drowning by a, er, juvenile gannet, who tossed him onto his back and paddled him all the way up the north coast to the cave below Tintagel Castle, where he was found by Merlin, and the rest is history. Dry valley indeed!

The headland was certainly a fortified settlement dating back 2000 years, but there is little evidence of permanent dwellings within the single rampart that was built across the wide neck of the promontory. Substantial remains of courtyard houses have been found close by, which were no doubt connected

Approaching Bosigran Castle. The ruined wall once supported a water-wheel which powered a series of stamps.

Looking across the Whirl Pool from Greeb Point. Bosigran Castle is in the distance.

The church at Morvah.

with the Iron Age fields still clearly in evidence along the coastal strip.

The valley leading to Porthmoina Cove played host to a vast array of mining hardware, although no mining of note took place here. The remains that can be seen today, thanks to the National Trust's clearance of the undergrowth, were concerned with the post-mining operations, buddling and calcinating (both processes will be explained later, when the coast path enters West Penwith's mining heartland). Suffice to say that these operations relied on flowing water to power the machinery, and any valley along the coast in this area that possessed a stream almost certainly housed similar processing equipment.

A slight detour from the path at this point will take you inland to the two engine houses of Carn Galver Mine. This was a relatively unsuccessful mine; it produced just 150 tons of tin in the 1860s and '70s. The engine houses were built in 1871, but by 1876 the mine had closed. The adit that drained the shaft at the mine is half a mile long and meets the coast at the back of Porthmoina Cove. The count house, adjacent to the engine houses, is now a lodging house for the Climbers Club of Great Britain.

Return to the coast and follow the cliff-top path. This stretch is known locally as Commando Ridge owing to the fact that, after the Second World War, Marine Commandos were trained here. Below you lie the Brandys, a small group of hazardous rocks which mark the entrance to the Whirl Pool. The cliffs above this inlet are especially beautiful and play host to some unusual rock formations that are covered with lichen. At low tide the sea reveals a golden beach, that is almost inaccessible. The name Whirl Pool derives from the action of the sea, as it eddies to and fro. In the shallow waters you can see how the sand is churned and a variety of sea birds swoop and dive to grab any food exposed as a result.

The path leads you past Trevowhan Cliff, across a small and overgrown stream and onto an open area that houses the last remnants of the numerous small mining operations in the area, known collectively as the Morvah Consols. This mine was active for several years between 1850 and 1880 and was last earmarked for reopening in 1928. The only production figures available concern the year 1873 when 6 tons of black tin were produced from the shaft that lies next to the dilapidated engine house. A little further along are the substantial remains of dressing floors. The watercourse the path crosses leading into the complex was without doubt the scene of tin streaming for many centuries prior to the existence of the consols.

The church, St Bridget of Sweden, was built in 1390 and was united with Madron at the beginning of the parochial system, one vicar attending both.

Morvah remains a separate parish, one of the smallest in Britain, and has registers dating back to 1617. The church was so named because of the popularity of the cult of the saint around the time it was built, and in 1427 a small religious foundation for Bridgettine nuns was established in the priory on St Michael's Mount. This makes the church special to the Swedish population of Britain, as it is the only one to have such a connection. Within the building are candlesticks, glassware and a Swedish flag donated by the Rotary club of Vadstena, the place in Sweden most associated with the saint.

The presence of the church indicates that the area had always been a religious centre and to the north-west sit the remains of an ancient baptistery or chapel, dating back to the time of the Celtic saints. These remains consist merely of large boulders, but the adjoining holy well is in good condition. Down the lane from the later church, and now part of a gate, stands the Giant Stone. This obelisk used to stand in the field parallel to the graveyard. The legend connected to it involved circling the stone nine times towards the sun. If you then dropped to your knees and put your ear to the ground you could hear a tinkling sound, as if someone were tapping a saucer with a spoon. On hearing the sound you were to make a wish, which would come true.

To the left the footpath follows another small stream that will eventually bring you out to the rear of Morvah church and into the village itself. Morvah was once a lot larger than it is today, populated by those who worked the Morvah Consols. The village covers approximately 2000 acres and stands 400ft above the sea.

Retrace your steps back down the path behind the church to the coast path and look eastwards over your shoulder – you will get a good view all the way back to Gurnard's Head. Above Trevean Cliff, Carn Galver looms through the haze on a hot sunny day. Cross over a large stone stile and with a little detour to the right you will be upon Chair Carn; a furze-capped rocky outcrop which in summer burns a fierce yellow against the grey of the granite.

Greeb Point is away down to the north. From your vantage point you may be lucky enough to spy gannets diving for fish. These birds spend most of their lives on the open sea, although the odd young bird can be seen straying inland. They breed on rocky shores and rock stacks, arriving in huge numbers between February and early April (one breeding area in the Outer Hebrides plays host to some 70 000 of them). Their nests are simple affairs, made up of seaweed and flotsam. The hen lays a single egg which is extremely thick shelled; the chick spends an entire day trying to hatch, and once out it spends the next eleven weeks being fed night and day by the parents. By the end of

The stream down the Portheras valley.

this period it weighs more than the adults and is turfed out of the nest unable to fly, but able to swim.

From the Chair Carn the path rejoins the main coast path that follows the wall of an ancient field. Cross another small wooden stile and on your right heather begins to take over from the furze as it fights for position with brackens and brambles. Over another stone wall and here the heather has won the day.

Somewhere amidst the thick carpet, which in the late summer turns a wonderful purple, sit the ruins of an ancient tumulus. Looking ahead, you will catch your first sight of Pendeen lighthouse, on the cliffs on the other side of Portheras Cove. Beyond this, the old stacks of the Levant and Geevor Mines can also be distinguished.

The path descends into Portheras valley. At the bottom of the hill turn right and make your way to the beach. At the valley bottom the path crosses the confluence of the Rose and Portheras streams. These steams provided the water that worked the stamping-mills further up the Portheras valley. There is little evidence of tin mining itself, but tin was brought here to be dressed. To satisfy demand water was diverted from the Rose stream, by way of leats, into the Portheras stream. Just above the confluence the remains of one of these leats can still be seen, although you will encounter better examples in the Kenidjack valley further along the way. There were eight stamping-mills in use at one time or another up the valley, and their remains can still be seen. At the mouth of the valley one was built as late as the 1920s.

The path crosses the stream, via stepping-stones (but prepare to get your feet wet if you arrive after a spell of heavy rain) and disintegrates a little as it approaches the beautiful but hazardous stretch of beach. Behind the sign warning not to walk barefoot or bathe, is clear evidence of the reason why. Buried in the sand are hundreds of razor-sharp fragments of metal, left over from a botched attempt at removing a shipwreck. At the back of the beach rise cliffs of head material (created by the intermittent thawing of the surface soil at the time of the ice age, head material slowly slid over the permafrost at the subsoil level, carrying with it many huge chunks of granite and greenstone) that look as though they may topple on your head at any moment. Out to sea is the hazardous Three Stone Oar reef, the presence of which, at high tide, is only given away by the breaking of the surf.

At the far end, if the tide is low, it may be possible to scramble over the rock and onto the slipway leading up to a few ramshackle net sheds. The path soon joins the gravel track that leads from the slip at the cove to Pendeen Watch.

Looking across Portheras Cove to Pendeen Watch.

5

BUSBY'S LEGACY

Trinity represents the oldest and most well-respected lighthouse authority in the world. The organisation was borne out of a charter granted by Henry VIII in 1514 to an ancient guild of mariners, the origins of which are unknown. The guild complained that there were no controls over the pilots, or leadsmen as they were called, who worked on the Thames. The charter gave the guild the controls they desired and they renamed themselves, rather gloriously, The Guild, Fraternity or Brotherhood of the Most Glorious and Unified Trinity and of St Clement in the Parish of Deptford Strand, latterly to be known as Trinity House. At the heart of this Corporation were the elder brethren: a master, wardens and assistants. The present master is the Duke of Edinburgh.

Pendeen Watch is the first of four lighthouses that are encountered along the path, not including the ones on the Scillies. The history of their construction is very interesting indeed: a mixture of heroism, folly, greed and philanthropy. Some were built by private individuals, others by Corporations, but all now operate under the stewardship of Trinity House.

In 1803, when Napoleon was eyeing the eastern seaboard of England, Trinity House undertook the defence of the Thames. It did this by mooring eleven frigates across the river at Lower Hope Reach.

Trinity's involvement with sea markers came through the renewal of a charter by Elizabeth I. The powers of the Corporation were extended to include the authority to erect beacons and set buoys to mark hazards at sea. No control was given, however, to the many privately owned lighthouses because the land rents from them were a lucrative source of revenue for the Crown. It was not until 1836 that Trinity was given the right to buy them, at a total cost of £1 200 000.

In the eighteenth and nineteenth centuries Trinity established thorough control of all the lighthouses and hazard markers throughout the British Isles, which, up to the late 1970s, included 90 lighthouses, 30 lightships, and nearly 700 buoys. A fleet of nine service ships was also maintained; each ship weighed over 2000 tons and had the capacity to haul a 10-ton buoy clear of the water in rough seas.

Pendeen Watch.

Penzance depot was founded in 1854 to provide a base for the construction of the Wolf Rock lighthouse. After it was completed the premises were purchased and converted to a buoy-maintenance depot, and a base for conducting relief for the Seven Stones lightship. The crews for the lightship and the keepers of the various lighthouses were all picked from the townsfolk.

Many would say that the influence of Trinity House helped steer the course of English history; it was certainly in the thick of any maritime incident that has occurred during the last 400 years. In 1588 the Corporation was instrumental, under the stewardship of Captain Salmon, in organising the flotilla of ships that defeated the Armada. The year 1632 saw Trinity lead an expedition to fight pirates off the Barbary Coast. A famous mutiny at the Nose, in 1797, saw the elder brethren sail to the Thames estuary to destroy all sea markers, in order to halt the mutineers who threatened to join the French and Dutch.

The first recorded wrecking on the rocks below Pendeen was of the *Naais*, a Rotterdam steamer that floundered off Morvah after being blown off course in June 1857. She was carrying a cargo of molasses and spirits and after running aground a battle apparently ensued between the militia and the local population, both keen to claim the booty that had been washed ashore. After the incident Trinity House looked into the possibility of erecting a warning beacon, but the deliberations eventually came to nothing. Over the next couple of decades further ships met similar fates. These included the 560-ton *Gannet* in 1871; a merchant ship from Bilbao in 1878; and the 580-ton coal ship *Alistair*.

The increasing regularity of mishaps galvanised Trinity House into action. A thorough investigation was commissioned into why so many wrecks were occurring in the region. The hazardous rocks that were causing so much devastation lay quite close to the cliffs, and Trinity House could see no reason why ships were coming to grief on them, especially when the main stretch of St George's Channel (the name given to the shipping lane that runs down the north coast of Cornwall) was safely navigable.

Entering Pendeen in the mid-nineteenth century.

After many weeks and no little expense James Nicholas Douglas, the man charged with investigating the phenomenon, came to the conclusion that between May and October (the months that saw the most wrecking incidents) the seas around Cape Cornwall were regularly shrouded in fog. Any local farmer or fisherman could have told the investigation that for free. Even in the winter months very few vessels were lost, so this summer fog was, correctly, deemed the source of the problem.

An incident involving the *Busby*, a steel-hulled schooner-rigged steamer, illustrates the hazardous nature of the sea fogs. The *Busby* was designed for trade between England and India. She had left Bristol on the morning of 26 June 1894 bound for Bombay. At 7.30pm she was sighted off Trevose Head near Padstow, the weather was clear and the sea was like a millpond. Rounding the peninsula her captain, as was regulation, altered course and set for the Longships lighthouse off Land's End. At 9.30pm the steamer was spotted off Godrevy Point. Within half an hour fog had rolled in and, as visibility dropped, the order was given for 'dead slow ahead'. As the ship felt her way through St George's Channel a lookout was set on the bow, and at 11.00pm he called out that he had seen a flash of light. The captain assumed this to be the flash of the Longships lighthouse and gave the order for 'full steam ahead.' Not long afterwards the *Busby* smashed into the Three Stone Oar reef, cutting a long gash in her stern. Most of the crew managed to escape by lowering the starboard lifeboats, but the captain and first officers, having stayed on board in an attempt to rescue the craft had to be rescued by a breeches buoy.

After Mr Douglas had conducted his investigation, the results, along with all the previous petitions from shipping merchants, were presented to the Board of Trade in October 1898. The department set about tendering for a building contract by advertising in the local press. The most favourable quote for the job

Evening on Pendeen Watch.

came from Arthur Carkeek & Co. of Redruth, and as the company had previously worked on breakwaters and harbour walls it was given the job of constructing the lighthouse.

To the rear of the tower the accommodation blocks were built to house the keepers and their families. A big problem was maintaining an adequate water supply, so the accommodation blocks were built with flat roofs, edged with a parapet to catch rainwater which was then channelled down to an underground storage tank. To the back of the blocks were long strip gardens. The idea was that the keepers would be able to grow their own fruit and vegetables, but as it turned out the dimensions proved very handy to hang out washing.

The first task facing the workers was to remove a hefty chunk of Pendeen Watch in order to create a level platform on which the tower and accompanying accommodation could be built. This was done by blasting, the product of which was used to build the enormous perimeter wall around the complex. As if to add impetus to the task, the work crew could only watch as, in January 1899, the 715-ton *Umbre* ran aground on Greeb Rocks.

Work on the tower began with the digging of a circular trench, to ensure the tower would be firmly anchored to the ground. Unlike the Herculean efforts involved in the constructions of the Wolf and Longships lighthouses, of which more later, the construction of the tower at Pendeen was incident free and completed within weeks. It finally reached a height of 33ft.

The strip gardens to the rear of the lighthouse.

The fresh sea air on the exposed headland had certainly put the wind in the sails of the lighthouse keepers; the first five years of them living there witnessed a population explosion. One keeper produced five children in quick succession, and soon the complex had the air of a small village community. Living within the perimeter wall were ten children, three wives, four keepers, two dogs, three cats, five pigs, three goats, two ponies, thirty chickens and three geese.

By the summer of 1900 most of the construction work had been completed. The Duke of York conducted the opening ceremony, unveiling a plaque amid the detritus of building tools and rubble that had not been cleared away for the royal visit. The tower and the buildings had not been painted either. When the huge job was finally finished the paint began to peel. It was redone in 1904, but the same thing happened. Then someone had the idea that, perhaps because the lighthouse was by the sea some salt-resistant paint might be needed.

The First World War saw the regular keepers called to arms, so men unable to fight because they were too old or infirm were given the job of tending the lanterns. One temporary keeper was unable to climb the stairs to get to the light gallery on account of his wooden leg. Needless to say there was a high turnover of staff during the conflict.

During this period, the keepers regularly reported hearing distant explosions as German U-boats claimed another merchant ship. By 1918 there were four subs known to be operating in the waters between Land's End and Pendeen. One particularly troublesome sub picked off the schooner *Moss Rose*, the 91-ton *Mary Orr*, the 197-ton frigate *Jane Williamson* and the 1417-ton steamer *Luxembourg*, all within an 8-mile radius of Pendeen. Of the 22 crew of the *Luxembourg*, 14 perished. They are buried in a mass grave at the church in Gwithian.

The road that leads from the car park at the back of Pendeen Watch will take you up to Pendeen. If you are in need of refreshment then no less than three pubs can be found here: The Radjel and The North are both on the main stretch, while The Trewellard Arms is a mile or so further along in the village of the same name. It is certainly worth walking a little way up the lane to see Pendeen Vau, the fogou that now forms part of a field wall at Portheras Farm. This fogou was first described by John Norden in the seventeenth century; he claimed that one of the most interesting things about it was the fact that the cavern changes direction halfway in. This relic has also been incorporated into a local fairytale.

Legend has it that a beautiful woman, dressed in white and clutching a red rose between her teeth, appears at the entrance of the chamber on Christmas morning. She is said to 'confide to you tidings brought from her native land through the submarine recesses of her dark cavern.' It is said that those who enter meet a horrible end. The ancients believed that for a mortal to enter the underworld before their allotted time, and return alive, it was necessary to carry a talisman or 'passport'. A red rose was a common passport carried by underworld travellers as it represented the sexual prowess of a goddess (red roses on St Valentine's day and all that). It is not accidental that the woman is said to appear on Christmas morning; the festival of Christmas has ties with a pagan mid-winter celebration that fell around the time of the winter solstice. The first dawn after the equinox represented a time of neither lengthening or shortening days, a state of limbo between the death and rebirth of the sun.

Looking across from Pendeen Watch to The Enys (centre) *and beyond to the Geevor and Levant Mines.*

From the road the path takes you across Pendeen Old Cliff and above The Enys, a great lump of killas cut from the mainland by the sea. The name Enys, encountered earlier in the walk at Pen Enys Point, is Cornish for 'remote island'. A little further along the Avarack, Cornish for 'fallow ground', protrudes from the cliff base. The land surrounding the path in this region is well vegetated, and hides much evidence of spoil heaps from the Boscaswell mines further inland. These were small enterprises and nothing compared to the works you are about to encounter as you make your way over Carn Ros and into the heartland of tin and copper mining on the peninsula.

From here all the way to Cape Cornwall, and a little way beyond, you will be walking through what was the economic powerhouse of West Penwith for nearly 300 years. Ahead of you lie the remains of the Geevor, Levant, Wheal Edward, Botallack, Cape Cornwall and St Just mining complexes.

6

LEAVE SOME OF THY FUGGAN FOR BUCCA

Several small tin-streaming operations had been registered in and around the Geevor complex as early as 1490, and a small mine called Wheal Geevor was operating just north of Levant in 1765. In 1851 all these operations were amalgamated under the name of North Levant, possibly in the hope that some of that great mine's fortunes may rub off. North Levant was only moderately successful, however, and it was closed in 1891. The following year it was reopened under the name Wheal Geevor, and for the next two decades the mine experienced a series of false dawns, as lode after lode was discovered, only to bring meagre rewards for the investors. In 1911 Geevor Tin Mines Ltd was created and the company embarked on a long period of expansion and modernisation. The main shaft for these operations was situated near the main entrance of the works and was named after Oliver Wethered, a long-serving director of the mine. For a while things ran well, as the turn of the century heralded a revival in tin prices, and a new shaft to the west was dug in 1919.

Geevor Mine complex.

The chequered history of Cornish mining has its basis in the free-spirited and independent nature of the Cornish themselves. When a lode of tin or copper was discovered the Cornish Adventurers, as these pioneers were known, tended to strike out on their own. They would invest considerable amounts of money on plant and machinery, hoping that the lode would be large enough to ensure some sort of return. Many abandoned mines were reopened again and again by a succession of optimists thinking that this time the shaft would be sunk in just the right place. Modern methods of quantifying and prospecting were absent so hundreds of mines in Cornwall came to very little by this hit-and-miss approach.

Geevor was one of the few mines in the west to survive the postwar depression and competition from the cheap foreign imports. By the 1950s it was still going, but beginning to run out of lodes to mine. The board of directors knew that rich seams still lay in the now-flooded shafts belonging to the long-extinct Levant workings that lay next to the site, so in the 1960s a five-year operation to seal off the old shafts and pump them free of water began. Concrete was used to plug the shafts and 50 000 000 gallons of water was pumped out, to a depth of 190 fathoms.

The lodes, when they were finally reached, proved disappointing and looked unlikely to yield anything like what was required to see a return on the huge investment. Yet more money was poured into the mine. In 1975 the shaft that had been dug in 1919 was extended deep under the sea. In 1980 work began on renewing some old Botallack workings, and by 1984 shafts had been dug to a depth of 2220ft, joined by over 100 miles of tunnels. Then in 1985 a worldwide slump in the price of tin shut down all operations. The water pumps were kept operating, however, and in 1987 the mine was opened once again, although not much was produced. Most of the money was earned by providing tourist trips down the shafts, to complement the museum that had been founded in 1977.

The mine finally bowed to the inevitable in 1990 when it closed for good. By the end of 1991 the pumps were switched off and the vast network of tunnels slowly flooded once more. The museum has been modernised and now delivers an excellent insight into this once-great industry.

Just take a couple of steps further along the path and you will come to the Levant Mine complex. Levant was known as a Champion Mine, and was worked for 110 years. Its location was determined 300 million years before when the granite intrusions of Land's End permeated the existing sedimentary rocks and extensive mineralisation occurred at the edges of the upsurge. Levant stands on the border between the granite and the killas. The principle minerals to be found within the greenstone are tin and copper with small occurrences of aragonite, bismuth, cobalt, fluorspar, garnet, gold, gypsum, iron, lead, quartz, silver, tourmaline, tungsten, uranium and zinc. The mine was formed from an amalgamation of the earlier pits, Zawnbrinney, Boscregan and Wheal Unity. In 1818, a group of 20 adventurers got together and formed a company that they divided into 80 shares. They soon struck a huge copper lode that in 1820 saw a total of £630 paid in dividends; a 1157 per cent return. By 1870 the mine had sold £1 million worth of ore.

The site of Levant Mine covers a half-mile stretch of coastline and runs about a quarter of a mile inland. The main tin-rich lodes worked ran north-west to south-east. The shafts were dug to follow the dip of these lodes, which fell away seaward, resulting in some extremely deep shafts. The deepest, dug in 1895, reached 350 fathoms. At 278 fathoms beneath the seabed a feature known as a carbona was found. This was a large irregularly shaped mass of mineral

Approaching Levant Mine from Geevor.

and was completely excavated in the early years of the nineteenth century, leaving a great cave. Despite being sunk almost entirely under the ocean, the mine had no great water problems; the killas and greenstone are watertight.

As the mine matured and the shafts were dug ever deeper, it became apparent that by the time the face workers had descended the shaft by ladder and walked nearly a mile further out under the sea, they were tired before their work began. The labour required for the ascents and descents were thought to contribute considerably to the increase in pulmonary diseases as the miners puffed and panted their way to and from the faces, inhaling the fines produced from the use of waterless pneumatic drills. In 1855 the introduction of a man engine hastened the decent considerably, yet the journey still took half an hour. The one used at Levant reached a depth of 266 fathoms.

Water may not have posed much of a problem to the miners but ventilation did. Temperatures at the deepest points could easily reach 82°F, and the movement of air was restricted by the lack of connecting shafts that would have allowed more circulation. Winzers were sunk between the levels and screens used to direct the draught from the air machines. These fans were turned by young boys who often sat in the pitch black for eight or nine hours at a time. Before Humphry Davy invented his lamp the standard form of illumination was a tallow candle stuck to a hardened felt hat by a lump of clay. An invisible danger was radon gas – although this was not recognised as such until thirty years ago, and most of the miners had already died of other causes by that time.

Levant in 2002.

At its height the mine had 96 stamp engines working the ore. The mine produced many metals, the most common being copper. Processing copper was a relatively simple operation; the ore was broken up and the waste rock was removed. A sieve was then used, within which the ore was jigged; the copper settled first. Extracting tin and the mixed ores involved a more complicated refining process, roughly divided into four parts. Buddling involved the use of a slime within which the ores were distributed via centrifugal forces according to the density of each piece. Calcinating was where the ores, most of which were sulphides, were fired in great furnaces to convert them to oxides. The resulting arsenic oxides were then condensed in extensive brick labyrinths (the one at Levant was called the Cathedral). The arsenic was then carried via horse and cart to Penzance for refining. Other oxides were buddled further. The copper oxides were treated with sulphuric acid in leaching tanks, then precipitated from solution by scrap iron. The fumes that belched from the chimneys were pretty nasty (the plant would have been shut down today) but soon dispersed on the almost constant winds.

Another invention that proved useful to miners was the safety fuse, invented by Solomon Bickford in 1831. Up to that point, and still after it really, blasting was a particularly dangerous part of the job; hollow reed stems filled with black powder were used as fuses and gave the blaster very little time to retreat to safety.

The workers themselves fell into two categories: tributers and tut-workers. The tut-workers were employed in the non-productive but essential side of operations, and were paid at a fixed price per fathom. Tributers were sub-contractors and the foreman of each gang would bid for a plot in the mine, which was priced at so much in the pound for the payable ore they sent to the surface. All were under the stewardship of the captains. These men were the middle managers on whom the smooth running of the mine depended. They took on the role of poacher turned gamekeeper; in other words they were usually once experienced face workers who knew the men and their needs, but also knew the scams they worked.

Bal maidens in their traditional working dress pose outside their mine, c.1890.

In the count houses were the officials. These men steered the mine through the trials and tribulations of an ever-fluctuating market; always looking out for fresh markets and uses for the ore. There were also many ancillary workers in and around the mine including blacksmiths, carpenters and engine drivers. They were able to charge their own rates for their services but pay for the miner was based on the price the mine received for its ore.

Records of 1837 show the miners of West Penwith had the lowest pay in the country. Tributers received 47s.6d., tut-workers 45s. and labourers such as bal maidens 42s. per month. In 1881, taking into account inflation, the price of tin was at a high, which was reflected in wages; tributers received £5.4.6d. However, only two years later, with another fall in the market, they only received £3.15s. per month. Considering what you could buy for £1 in those days this was a huge drop in pay, especially so when many of the miners' fellow countrymen were earning £120 per month in the mines of South Africa.

Militancy was in a healthy state at Levant. There was a strike over pay in 1870. In 1882 there was a dispute over the quality of the candles used in the helmets, and another one over the quality of the dynamite. The concept of time-keeping was particularly abhorrent to the Cornish, so there was another strike over the imposition of a time register at the shaft head in 1892.

Knocking-off time would bring with it the amazing and, no doubt, rather eerie sound of the men singing their way up the shaft on the man engine. The sound of the impromptu male voice choir echoing out of the chambers of an evening must have been something to hear. As in Wales, male voice choirs abound all over Cornwall and were recruited from the region's industries.

You made your own entertainment in these desolate areas. Going to the pub was the favourite pastime of many, though church events such as outings, fêtes and feasts were well attended. Once a week a horse bus ran from St Just to Penzance.

Tragedy was also a constant companion to these communities. Levant's most infamous accident occurred on 20 October 1919. That afternoon a full shift returned to the surface on the man engine. Fully laden, the device was carrying an extra 24 tons. However, the conveyer, holding 36 men, had not returned to the surface; instead it had fallen 46 fathoms. The last body was brought out of the mine five days after the disaster, giving testimony to the enormous problems facing the rescuers, who had to climb down the cliffs and enter via an adit. The inquest gave a verdict of accidental death. The cause of the accident was put down to a flaw in the manufacture of the device. A memorial tablet stands in the chapel at Trewellard at the top of Levant Road. The disaster marked the beginning of the end for the mine. A crash in tin prices, to only £99 per ton after the First World War, followed by a general worldwide economic slump saw the mine finally close in 1930.

Leaving the Levant Mine complex.

The Levant complex is now under the stewardship of the Trevithick Trust, named after the Cornish engineer Richard Trevithick (1771–1833). Founded in 1993 the Trust's aim is to restore and preserve Cornish industrial-heritage sites. Other such sites under their care include the Museum of Submarine Telegraphy at Porthcurno and Pendeen Watch.

As the path leaves the Levant Mine complex it splits in two. The right-hand track leads to the cliff edge and involves some hairy moments as the path seems to disappear in places, leaving you to scramble rather like a mountain goat over the rocky peaks. The effort is well worth it, however, as the left-hand track although being easier, takes you across some pretty barren scenery as nature fights for a way through the desolation left by mining activity.

Crossing more spoil heaps will eventually bring you to a fantastic opportunity to inspect a mine shaft up close. This one has been capped with a metal grill, so anyone with a head for heights can walk across the grill over the yawning chasm. The site is bounded by an incredible wall that rises almost from the sea itself. A small climb past yet more mine waste will bring you to the top of Botallack Head. From here you get a good view across De Narrow Zawn and Zawn a Bal, to the ancient stronghold of Kenidjack Castle, which lies ahead. At the far edge of Botallack Head there is a bird's-eye view of the famous, and oft-photographed Crown Mines, nestled on the ledge below. Beyond are the engine houses of the Wheal Edward mine.

As you pass the remains of the munitions store for the mine, glance over your shoulder to see the Levant and Geevor complexes. Skirting Levant Zawn the path drops to the sea a little and on your left lies an old stone quarry. Keep an eye out for adits; peer inside one of these and the ground water level is visible. The path throws up a multitude of possible ways forward, but take the far-right one again. This will lead you to the small summit that is Carn Vellan which allows you a good look ahead at the spectacular coastal scenery; you will get your first proper view of The Brisons, lying off Cape Cornwall. Take time to inspect the detail in the metamorphosed sedimentary rock. Each layer of sediment, some only a few millimetres thick, deposited when this ground was the ocean floor, can be easily determined. You will enter a small inlet known as Stamps an Jowl Zawn. The path skirts this cove taking you across a huge mine-spoil dump, created by decades of back-breaking work by bal maidens (usually women who worked the ore with spalling hammers into smaller pieces to aid separation and improve the grade quality). The far side of the Zawn gives you a good view of the small natural arch, lying below the route you have just taken.

Opposite: *The Crown Mines at Botallack.*

The area covered by the Botallack Mine complex represents the earliest site of mining activity in Cornwall. John Norden wrote in 1594 'Botallack [is] most visited with tinners where they lodge and feed near their mines'. He makes no mention of mines at Pendeen or St Just and the workings he describes here were small enterprises that were combined under the name Botallack.

The Prince of Wales' party at Botallack.

One of the first mines to explore the deeper lodes was Wheal Cock, which had driven levels deep under the ocean as early as 1778. Here miners experienced the deep thundering roar of the Atlantic over their heads as it moved huge boulders over the sea floor. It was later discovered that some of the shafts were dug so that only just over a metre of rock remained between the ceiling and the ocean floor. Late in the 1840s the mine was gradually extended and the famous Boscawen diagonal shaft, the mouth of which is marked by the uppermost Crown engine house, was dug in 1858. The two spectacularly situated engine houses contained a whim engine, housed in the higher building, and a beam engine in the lower.

Late in the 1860s a slump in the price of tin threatened the mine's existence, but it survived by retrieving and selling arsenic. The calciners used for the process are sited above the mine on the cliff path. The winter of 1894–95 saw massive flooding around the mine and the subsequent loss of working weeks forced the shareholders to sell almost all of the surface plant to avoid bankruptcy. The last miners left the area in 1914. In 1985 the dilapidated engine houses were restored by the Carn Brea Mining Society.

The opening of the railways from the east made this site one of the first tourist destinations in the far west. Some of the miners complained that their work was constantly interrupted when they were required to give the *hoi polloi* guided tours of the shafts, something for which they were not paid. Edward Prince of Wales (and Duke of Cornwall) paid a visit in 1865 and bravely made the descent and ceremoniously dug a little of the vein stone some 1358ft under the sea. The writer and poet Wilkie Collins was a later visitor and he describes in great detail the naked fear he felt as he made the descent.

Knockers, or Nuggies as they are sometimes known, are the spirits of ancient miners and are said to haunt the shafts and adits of the mines in this area. Too bad to go to heaven, but not quite evil enough for hell, these old, small and wizened spooks spend their time in the nether world causing a menace. Said to be big of head and ungainly of limb, they can be spiteful when angered; miners' whistling and cursing underground was strictly forbidden for fear of annoying the Knockers. Miners in the nineteenth century would swear blind (though not within earshot of the spirits) that they heard the ghostly tapping of tiny pickaxes whenever a rich seam was about to be unearthed. Many others would leave a little of their croust (supper) in the mine when they left, for the Knockers to munch; it was believed this would bring good luck.

One man who paid no heed to the rantings of superstitious old men was Tom Treverro from St Just. He had no time for tall tales of small spirits; he was a rough, tough miner, thick of fetlock and firm of buttock. He wasn't going to leave any of his hard-earned croust behind for those devils to eat.

Tom Treverro, Tom Treverro
Leave some of thy fuggan for bucca
Or bad luck for thee tomorrow.

Tom had been working down the Bellowall Mine when the voices had begun. But he put them down to the echoes created by the dripping of sea water through the tunnel's ceiling.

Tom Treverro, Tom Treverro
We'll send thee bad luck tomorrow
Thou Old curmudgeon to eat thy fuggan
And not leave a didjun for bucca.

Tom was not only dismissive of the Knockers, he was also a lazy soul, although his brother, Billy, was neither. The next day while Tom slept Billy discovered a rich seam of diamonds in the mine, no mean feat in a land of tin. The Knockers appeared and instructed Billy to fill his bags with as much as he could carry. He did so, and being a generous soul, he went home to share the booty with his brother. Tom however, wanted more so went to the mine to dig his own diamonds. He found the seam and filled his bags, but as he climbed to the surface his ladder began to collapse, along with the shaft it was propped up against. In order to save his life he had to let go of his bags. As he scrambled to the shaft head the ladder gave way and the walls of the shaft buried it and his diamonds forever. Tom was saved by the strong hand of Billy that reached down and plucked him from certain death. From deep underground there was a faint whispering:

Tom Treverro, Tom Treverro
We sent thee bad luck
And we'll send thee some more tomorrow...

Botallack Mine, mid-1800s.

Tom lived the rest of his days in foreign climes, hoping to escape the curse of the Knockers. In South America, in Australia, wherever he mined, disaster lay just around the corner for him, and he died a very poor man.

Leaving the Botallack Mine complex the path leads you through the Wheal Edward Mine and the remains of yet more engine houses. If you were to keep to the track it would eventually bring you out on the main St Just road, but a signposted right turn takes you across the cliff tops once more. The path cuts through some thick furze and then brings you to within sight of Kenidjack Castle. The promontory the site covers is a mish-mash of various human enterprises that span some 2000 years; it once played host to a castle, a battery, a quarry and more tin mining.

The stone quarry was once linked to the main road by a tramway. Along it the granite was transported for use in buildings around the peninsula. The ruined building above the great hole may have been the quarry manager's house, although some believe it has more to do with St Just Battery, stationed here between 1870 and the early 1900s. The firing positions can still be made out; the gun emplacements are visible in the cement.

The area hit the news in the early 1990s when the local council tried to evict a group of settlers that had made the place their home. Public opinion was apparently on the side of the settlers, but the powers that be had their way and the site was eventually cleared.

A Bronze Age circle is also visible, with a burial mound at its centre. It was no doubt connected to the Cliff Castle that occupied the headland here. The remains of the small settlement connected with the castle were lost when the quarry was dug, but on the eastern side of the headland a triple rampart can still be seen which acted as the outer defences to the stronghold. About 100yds outside the entrance two bronze axes were found, dating back to the period the castle was occupied. They were found to contain 17 per cent tin which would have made them too brittle for use in combat. Perhaps their owners discovered that the hard way.

It is thought that the castle here, and the one at the Cape, protected the valuable tin and copper deposits that lay in Porth Ledden between them. These deposits were washed down by the stream from the valley, and there is little doubt that the local populace mined them; the castles mark the beginning of an ancient track along which the metals were transported to the harbours on the other side of the peninsula from where they would have been exported.

A small path leads to the end of the headland which then takes you back above Zawn Buzz. The Kenidjack valley appears below, across which is a

Looking to Cape Cornwall from Kenidjack across Porth Ledden.

Cape Cornwall from a Victorian print.

Opposite: *Looking back to Kenidjack Castle from Cape Cornwall.*

spectacular view of Cape Cornwall, The Brisons beyond and, on a clear day, the Longships and Wolf Rock lighthouses in the far distance. There are two possible routes down. To the left the path leads up the valley and is a pleasant stroll. This route will give you the chance to inspect at close quarters some of the best preserved calciners and stamping-mills in Cornwall. The valley played host to the Boswedden Mine formed through the amalgamation of several smaller tin and copper works.

The stream that flows down the valley, variously called the Kenidjack, Tregeasel, Nancherrow or Boswedden, was vital for the operation of the numerous mills, stamps and dressing floors. It is said that as it flowed into the valley it was crystal clear, but by the time it reached the sea after having been used and reused, it stained the sea a deep red. By no means big, this stream was utilised to operate over 50 water-wheels. At its bottom lie the remains of one of these wheel pits (the best preserved in Cornwall) which gives some indication of the size of the wheels that were used.

Looking up the side of the valley, on the Cape Cornwall side, the well-preserved remains of leats can clearly be seen. These diverted the stream water to drive the wheels further up the valley side. The top leat ran round to Cape Cornwall Mine and powered the stamps there. At the top of the valley there are the remains of the calciners of the Kenidjack arsenic works. In 1892 a flash flood that followed a big freeze saw much of the plant destroyed and many jobs were lost for good as the mine never really recovered following a drop in tin prices. There is a small derelict building down by the beach that has nothing to do with mining. It housed a water turbine, known as a pelton wheel, which provided electricity for the old Cape Cornwall Hotel. The rusty remains of the old petrol turbine can still be seen.

If you have had your fill of tin extraction, then a steep and tricky descent will bring you to the mouth of the valley and the northern side of Porth Ledden. At low tide, and taking great care, it is possible to cross the boulder-strewn cove to reach the small slipway on the far side. However, if rock hopping is not your thing then cross the stream and follow the old leats until you reach the neck of the Cape.

Kenidjack Mine complex looking from up the valley.

7
A NEW OCEAN

What makes a cape, a cape? Cape Horn and the Cape of Good Hope mark the points where the Atlantic Ocean meets the Pacific, in the case of the former, and the Atlantic joins the Indian Ocean in the latter. Although there is still much debate, Cape Cornwall represents the point where the St George's Channel meets the English Channel. Some may tell you that this event actually occurs at Gwennap Head, further round the peninsula. Others say it is at Land's End. But for the sake of a quiet life this book shall go with the generally held belief that the two seas meet here, at Cape Cornwall.

The Cape was undoubtedly home to a cliff castle – up until the middle of the nineteenth century defensive ramparts could clearly be seen on the neck of the headland but ploughing has obliterated them over the years. Next to these defences a number of round barrows and burial mounds have also been identified, which unfortunately met a similar fate.

Before the chimney-stack was erected a beacon and watch-tower stood on the summit to warn ships of The Brisons, but it is now difficult to imagine the Cape without its familiar chimney. It has stood here for over a century and a half. It was originally connected via a long flue to a whim engine house below on the eastern cliff, but the draught it created was too great for the boiler so a smaller chimney was built just above the engine house, making the great stack obsolete. Still, it looks impressive and has proved an invaluable navigation aid for shipping; indeed, this was the main reason it was not demolished.

Looking into Priest's Cove on the southern side of the Cape you may notice a distinct change in the rock; here is the dark Devonian sediment, which contrasts with the granite cliffs on the north side of the Cape. The two rock types make contact right through the middle of the headland where a mineralised lode exists, and where there's a lode there is, of course, a mine.

The Cape Cornwall Mine began life in 1836 and was worked until 1875. Old photographs show a similar scene to that at Botallack, with the engine houses crouching on the cliff edge at the end of the Cape. The buildings on the

Cape Cornwall.

Looking inland from the Cape.

The south side of the Cape: Priest's Cove.

St Helen's Oratory.

road leading to the summit are the old count houses. The remains below them towards Priest's Cove are of an old vinery.

Hidden below the chimney-stack is a National Coastwatch Institute station. It is the most westerly station the NCI operates and has been in use since May 1996. The busy Land's End traffic is monitored from here.

On the eastern side of the Cape is the tiny chapel known as St Helen's Oratory, of which very little now remains. In the mid-nineteenth century a cross with a Chi Rho monogram was discovered in a leat by John Buller, then vicar of St Just. It was then, allegedly, thrown down one of the wells of the vicarage by his successor. The Chi Rho is one of the most ancient 'sacred monograms' of Christ, developed by early Christians as a secret sign of faith. It is generally formed of the Greek letters chi (X) and rho (P), the first letters of the Greek word 'XPICTOC', pronounced Christos, which of course means Christ. The monogram has been styled in a variety of ways over the centuries.

Priest's Cove, or the cove of St Just, is a popular site in the summer. Although there is no beach, a small bathing pool allows children to swim in comparative safety. To the south three adits can be seen in the cliffs and immediately to the south of these is a hole which formerly held a water-wheel. The wheel was used in the early 1800s to help pump what was then called Little Bounds Mine. Between the adits and the high-water mark a stream of water reveals where the miners broke into the cove from below. The hole was filled with timbers which were caulked with tar, like a ship's bottom, to make it waterproof.

Cape Cornwall was gifted to the nation, under the stewardship of the National Trust, by H.J. Heinz Ltd in 1987. It was formerly owned by Francis Oats, who built the large house that later became the Cape Cornwall Hotel, which overlooks the headland.

Oats worked at the Botallack Mines when he was still a child. Later he moved to South Africa and became the chairman of the De Beers Company and an active member of the Cape Legislative Assembly. He helped organise the civil defence force during the Boer Wars. It was probably his love of the Cape of Good Hope that inspired him to purchase Cornwall's somewhat smaller version in his autumn years.

Ballowall Barrow.

There are a number of tracks leading out from the Cape but all eventually lead to a rough track going up to Carn Gloose. This is a pleasant picnic site and indeed one or two benches and tables have been conveniently installed.

On the road that eventually leads to St Just sits the mysterious Ballowall Barrow (pronounced Bal-Owl). This barrow was located right in the middle of the St Just United Mine – although the original architects were not to know that of course – and as a result it was buried beneath tons of mine waste. It was rediscovered by a W. Copeland Borlase, a descendant of the famous antiquarian William Borlase. Ballowall may date back to the Neolithic or early Bronze Age (2500–1500BC) or possibly a little later (some pottery found within suggests 1500–500BC). The central chamber was thought to originally have had a domed roof and contained several stone coffins. The surrounding walls, up to 8ft high and 20ft thick, were added at a later date. The main entrance to the barrow does not line up with the rising or setting sun on ceremonial dates (such as the solstice or equinox) so a connection with the moon has been suggested. Borlase directed the excavation in the late 1870s, during which much rebuilding was done, including raising the central wall so the main chamber could be viewed more easily.

Looking back across the Cape from Carn Gloose.

The face of the cliff on the right is a perfect geological record of the last 100 million years. Towards the bottom is a raised beach below which is a series of slates with granite intrusions that were formed in stages over the last one million years, when the sea was 26ft higher than at present. The upper section consists of head material.

The Brisons seen from Porth Nanven.

Down on the beach The Brisons lay dead ahead of you, slowly being worn down by the interminable sea. In rough weather this is a good place to watch them get a hammering from the surf and it is interesting to hear, during an onshore wind, the slight time delay between seeing a breaker hit the rocks and actually hearing it.

The wave-worn granite boulders on the shore are some of the smoothest you will see anywhere along the coast – so much so that they often proved irresistible to walkers looking to use them as garden ornaments. A few years ago it was discovered that a city in the north of England was using a considerable number of the stones, taken from this very beach, in one of their town-centre displays. A stern letter of rebuke was sent by Penwith Council for this act of 'vandalism'.

Ballowall Mine, later united with the St Just Consols, stretched from the coast all the way along the north side of the Cot Valley. This area was mined in prehistoric times and was still being worked in the 1940s. In this relatively small area some 106 shafts were sunk, along with a total of 17 adits to drain them of water. Much of the area is overgrown so a careful step is required as you pick your way along the cliff top inland, until the path takes you down the north face of Cot Valley and out to Porth Nanven.

If you arrive in Porth Nanven during an onshore breeze the first thing that may hit you is the smell. Running along the right of the cove, as you look at the sea, is a raw sewage pipe that discharges about half a mile out. Sounds pretty vile but it does not harm the natural environment and it is screened for other waste before it is discharged. It just whiffs a bit, that's all.

Leading inland from the boulder beach is Cot Valley, an area rich in the remains of dressing floors and stamping-mills. Explore this valley as further on it is very pretty, but once you've seen one set of ruined dressing floors, you've seen 'em all! The path that leads out of Porth Nanven crosses the stream opposite a car park and up over a small carn. It passes a number of adits in the cliffs. These run very deep and eventually connect with a number of shafts, so do not enter them on any account.

From here on you are treated to spectacular views of Cape Cornwall (behind) and Land's End. As you approach Gribba Point the path begins to rise to a grassy plateau, used as rough grazing for cattle. You will pass Polpry Cove, scrambling over Carn Polpry as you go, and the shattered rocky outcrop of Maen Dower, where you have the chance to venture closer to the sea and spend time on a beautiful grassy meadow.

From Maen Dower the path disappears and allows you to wander unfettered across rolling grassland. A small stile at the far end of these fields marks the start of the beautiful National Trust-owned Nanjulian Cliff. This coastal region was also once home to a small number of dressing floors and a wheel pit that powered stamps, buddles and settling tanks. The plant was utilised by the Boscregan Mine and a collection of smaller enterprises that came and went over the years.

From Nanjulian the path sits quite low at the base of the cliffs and rounds Aire Point. You are now in Whitesand Bay; a vast swathe of golden sand, or at high tide, two smaller beaches (although they are still by far the biggest on the peninsula). These are Gwynver Beach immediately ahead and Sennen Cove in the distance.

These beaches are a favoured destination for an ever-increasing number of surfers. Gwynver in particular sees some of the best surf around, although it can be a pretty hair-raising experience owing to the hazardous rocks that protrude into the bay at the far end. A low cliff will take you round to the sand, but at low tide it is worth taking a small detour to the rock pools to see what aquatic life the tide has left behind. Both beaches can be very busy in the summer months.

The shafts and adits as you leave Porth Nanven.

Whitesand Bay from Nanjulian Cliff.

Gribba Point.

Gwynver Beach.

Whitesand Bay.

The sloping cliffs above Gwynver play host to some ancient terraced fields. These are difficult to make out in the summer months due to the undergrowth, but in winter the boundary walls stand proud as if they had been built yesterday. A good vantage point from which to see them is the top of the wooden steps that lead from the back of the beach.

Gwynver is the more isolated of the two beaches and access to it from Sennen Cove is via the path that skirts the small headland between them, although at low tide it is possible to walk the entire stretch of beach from Gwynver to Sennen Cove uninterrupted.

If you arrive in the area at high tide then the path to Sennen Cove follows Escalls Cliff, across the first stretch of the mountainous sand-dunes that have accumulated over centuries and out onto the second beach.

8

LEAN ON THE WINDLASS AND THINK ABOUT BOATS

The region of ocean that lies between the Runnel Stone (south of Gwennap Head) and Longships is known to fishermen as the Throes. This is where the two opposing ocean currents battle it out for supremacy. Out of the west the tidal stream flows from the St George's Channel and runs in a south to south-westerly direction and collides with the ebb tide of the English Channel coming from the east. In rough weather this phenomenon produces very dangerous and choppy seas known as 'pooks'. Take a trip on the *Scillonian* from Penzance to the Isles of Scilly and, even on calm days, your stomach will let you know that you have cleared Land's End and are in the Throes; the *Scillonian* is not known as the 'Great White Stomach Pump' for nothing.

Another hazard for mariners around these waters is the wind. During the normal course of a cyclonic weather system the winds will veer quite suddenly from a south-westerly direction to a north-westerly one; one minute pushing ships, especially in the days of sail, either onto the rocks of Cornwall's north coast, or swinging them round into the long arm of the Lizard peninsula. Throw in a sudden summertime sea fog, as the warm south-west breezes collide with the cold waters off the western extremities of Cornwall, and it comes as no surprise that between Tol-Pedn-Penwith and Gurnard's Head lie over 130 recorded shipwrecks, and no doubt countless more that have gone unrecorded. A veritable haven amongst these various jaws of death is Sennen Cove.

The village is situated on the southern extremity of Whitesand Bay and, because of its reputation for being the only place to land a sizeable ship between St Ives and Newlyn, it has seen some pretty significant incidents through the course of history.

Some of the earliest 'visitors' to the cove did not have frolicking on the golden sands in mind when they landed. On reaching the beach at Gwynver they proceeded inland, and for the next two days pillaged their way across the peninsula. The story of what happened next is a fine example of the way fact and fantasy combine to produce a jolly good yarn, and brings us to our second encounter with King Arthur. The story goes thus: panic stricken, the

Sennen Cove.

inhabitants of the peninsula settlements lit a series of beacons set in a line on the highest points of the region, such as Chapel Carn Brea, Sancreed Beacon and Trencom Hill. These fires led all the way to Tintagel Castle near Bude, where Arthur held court, and informed him of the attack.

The speed at which Arthur arrived at the scene suggests he may have already been in the area, quite possibly at his summer hunting lodge at Treryn Dinas, Porthcurno. On arrival he was supported by eight other important kings or tribal chiefs of Cornwall. The ensuing battle of Velan Druchar, popularly thought to have been to the east of St Buryan, ended in the invaders being routed and forced back into the ocean from whence they came. The victorious kings held a banquet at Table Maen, a flat-topped rock of which there were many used for such purposes dotted around Cornwall. The dates given for this conflict vary, but it most likely took place between AD450–650. This being so, the invaders were probably Angles, Saxons or Jutes checking out the area with a view to settling.

Athelstan, who came to the thrones of Wessex and Mercia in AD924 before becoming King of England a year later, landed in the cove during his reign (AD925–39), at the beginning of his campaign to annex Cornwall. King Stephen (c.1097–1154, grandson of William the Conqueror) also chose this site as the scene of his arrival from the Continent in order to claim the English throne before his aunt Matilda. Another future king who used the bay, although in this case it was to beat a hasty retreat, was the son of Charles I who reportedly stayed at Nangalyan Farm (believed to be between Sennen and Land's End) the night before sailing for the Scillies. However, his last night must have been a rather sleepless one as two other places profess to have played host to him – he must have moved around a bit!

In his book *The English Riviera*, written in 1912, J. Harris Stone said of the folk at Sennen:

> ... the men have one absorbing interest that keeps them occupied. The whole day long they are cleaning boats, patching boats, rowing boats, or lounging by the windlass at the top of the little cove looking at boats, with their hands in their pockets and pipes in their mouths, thinking of boats.

Indeed fishing was just about the be all and end all of things for many years, although Sennen bears little resemblance to the traditional Cornish fishing harbour. It is not even a cove in the usual sense. To the east and west of Whitesand Bay the granite cliffs stand hard and impregnable, whereas the bay

The Back.

has a softer appearance; the build up of sand has created rolling dunes that meet a low cliff of head material, above which rises a steep grassy hillside.

The harbour was constructed to facilitate hauling boats clear of the winter seas, a task that was first done by hand. In the late 1880s a 30ft-wide channel was cleared of boulders for the purpose and many of the rocks were utilised in the construction of the low breakwater known as The Back. Above the high-water mark the low head cliff was cut back to make way for a slipway of flat granite blocks. At its head a large capstan was constructed to make the job of hauling the boats up the slip easier. To the west a wharf was built to make access to the slip easier but the lack of a sizeable breakwater was still a problem. The breakwater seen here today, in a rough ocean, takes a particular hammering from the 'great mother sea' and it is easy to imagine just what difficulties the fishermen faced launching their boats before it was built.

Colonel H.W. Williams JP headed the board of inquiry into a solution and was instrumental in raising £3500 for the construction of the breakwater that was to eventually allow the unhindered launching of boats from the cove in all weathers. The breakwater allowed fishermen to catch the first influx of grey mullet arriving into the coastal waters in the early spring, when the weather was often still inclement. The cove marked the northern limit of the pilchard feeding grounds; these fish arrived off Sennen in July. Also throughout the summer months shellfish – primarily crab and lobster – provided the staple catch, and a bonanza could usually be predicted year in year out, for there was little local competition. Porthgwarra was the nearest fishing cove of any note. Still the 1880 season saw a lean time and trouble soon flared up with the Sennen fishermen threatening to shoot anyone, notably Porthgwarra and Priest's Cove men, casting their nets in Sennen's waters.

The Back does its job.

Seine-netting was an expensive business. A seine boat was over 30ft long with a 12ft beam, while the nets were usually 300 fathoms long, 7 fathoms deep, and weighed over 3 tons. Men known as 'huers' would direct the men controlling the nets towards shoals of pilchards, from high on the surrounding cliffs, signalling their instructions with furze bushes. A support boat and processing buildings on the shore also had to be financed. The car park adjacent to the capstan gallery now stands on the site of a thatched pilchard press. After the First World War the seine industry collapsed and only summer shellfish fishing remained, as it does to this day, albeit on a much smaller scale.

In the 1870s there were two seine-nets working out of Sennen Cove; the poor-man's seine, owned by the local fishing families, and the rich-man's seine, owned by the Chenells family, trading as The Sennen Fishing Co. This family was so rich that they even had a steam engine in their boat which gave them considerable advantage over their poorer rival.

The weather in west Cornwall is, at best, unpredictable. It does not behave properly until it hits Camborne; until then it is not sure whether it is over the ocean or over land. A well-known saying in the region is 'If you can see the Lizard it's going to rain, if you can't it's raining'.

Other local sayings:

Mist from the sea
Brings fine weather to thee;
Mist From the hills
Brings water for mills.

Rainbow to windward, foul fall the day;
Rainbow to leeward, damp runs away.

A fog and a small moon
Brings an easterly soon.

The fishermen of old often encountered the Hooper, a dense sea fog that would suddenly roll into shore. They believed this mist contained a spirit that warned of coming stormy weather, and those who dared ignore the spirit's warning and put to sea were met with a resistance from the fog. Two fishermen who did so entered the fog and were never seen again. Once more, this tale has a firm basis in fact. A sudden dense fog along the coast after a spell of fine weather usually indicates the forward edge of an approaching weather system. However, the fate of these two particular fishermen is certainly a mystery.

At the end of the foreshore road stands the recently modernised lifeboat station. The cove is the ideal launch site for lifeboats as it is well sheltered in rough seas. The incident that highlighted the need for a lifeboat in the area was the wrecking in 1852 of the *New Commercial*, a brig from Whitby. She was sailing from Liverpool to the Spanish Main when she came to grief on a ledge off The Brisons and began to break up. The skipper, Captain Saunders, along with his wife and eight hands, managed to scramble from the wreck and onto the rocks but a wave overwhelmed them and they were swept back into the sea. Seven of the seamen perished but the captain and his wife managed to

The church at Sennen.

struggle back to Little Brison and hang on. Meanwhile the remaining seaman had constructed a raft out of driftwood and canvas, which enabled him to navigate out of the hazardous seas to the relative calm of Whitesand Bay where he was rescued by Sennen fisherman. Captain George Davies R.N., inspecting commander of coastguards, ordered the revenue cutter *Sylvia* to round Land's End and attempt to rescue the captain and his wife, clinging for dear life on the rock. He watched from Cape Cornwall as repeated attempts failed due to the worsening conditions. As night fell the rescue was called off.

The next morning conditions were somewhat calmer so six boats were dispatched to try another rescue. Captain Davies, on the lead boat, fired a powerful line rocket by hand, without any protection from the tremendous kickback, and eventually managed to get a line to the couple. Captain Saunders tied the line around his wife's waist and told her to jump. She hesitated a moment too long, however, and jumped straight into a succession of breaking waves, putting all in perilous danger. After much struggling she was finally hauled aboard but tragically died a short time later. Captain Saunders survived. Davies and the commander of the *Sylvia* were awarded the RNLI's gold medal for their part in the action. The lasting legacy of the incident was the installation of a lifeboat at Sennen.

In 1852 the National Shipwreck Institution delivered a six-oared lifeboat, brought by steamer to Penzance, then towed to Sennen. The boat only saw one act of service in May 1856 before it was replaced in 1864 by a ten-oared self-righting boat called the *Cousins William and Mary Anne*, financed by a Mrs Mary Anne Davies whose husband's name was George. This lifeboat saw action off The Brisons when the *Devon* was dashed against the rocks with the loss of 17 out of the 18 crew. The one survivor, the mate, leapt out on the seaward side of the floundering vessel and was able to scramble to safety on the rocks where he was picked up. His name was later given as George Davies.

The early lifeboats of Sennen were launched from the back of a horse-drawn carriage that was backed up to the shoreline on the beach. In 1879 a boat-house was constructed on the present site and a new lifeboat, the *Denzil and Maria Ounslow,* was installed. It was involved in a rescue in 1891 and is noteworthy because, as a result of the rough conditions, many of the regular crew refused to man the boat, so a call was put out for volunteers. An artist, a barrister and a stockbroker duly came forward and in near-hurricane conditions found the abandoned ship in the Bristol Channel. No survivors were discovered and the lifeboat was forced to land in St Ives.

The lifeboat and quick-response craft today.

The next boat, the *Anne Newbon,* had a particularly distinguished career. In 22 years she saved 132 lives from a variety of vessels including naval ships and a sea plane. In 1896 a new boat-house was constructed which incorporated sliding doors and a slip. Next to the boat-house a carriage house was built which still allowed for the old delivery style if the need arose.

In 1929 a higher and larger boat-house was completed with a launch and recovery slipway and a turntable inside. The crew of the *Newbons* managed to save the lives of 36 mariners in all. It served the cove throughout the war years.

After the war the *Susan Ashley* replaced the *Newbons.* The lifeboat *Diana White* arrived in Sennen in 1974, complete with the latest equipment that included echo sounding and radar. She also had better protection for the crew against the elements. In turn, the *Diana White* was replaced in 1991 by the *Four Boys,* which saw service for seven years. In 2003 the lifeboat serving out of the cove is the *RNLB Norman Salveson,* a 47ft steel self-righting boat, powered by two 525hp GM Diesel engines. She has a top speed of 18 knots, which can be maintained for 10 hours. Also on standby is an inshore lifeboat, *The Spirit of the ACC.* With a crew of three this boat is a fast-response craft capable of 20 knots,

The annual gig-racing world championships on the Scillies.

and is used in close-to-cliff rescues in a medium surf. The station from which the boats are launched is unique in the fact that it has two slipways. The smaller of the two allows the boats to be retrieved in the shelter of the breakwater at high tides, while the larger allows retrieval and launching at low tides.

Another type of boat common in the waters around Cornwall was the pilot gig, crewed by men who knew the local waters well because their original purpose, as their named suggests, was to guide those larger vessels, whose captains were uncertain of hidden dangers such as stacks and reefs, into harbour. The larger harbour villages sometimes had more than one gig for the job, so whichever boat arrived at an approaching ship first would get the job, and the payment. As ocean charts became more detailed, and sonic radar more refined, the need for pilot gigs diminished, but the traditions associated with the boats has lived on. The most obvious one is gig racing, where boats from neighbouring harbours compete against each other for the local cup. In 1989 the world championships for gig racing was started on the Scillies (the islands probably have more gigs per square mile than any other place in the world). Every year around Easter gigs from as far afield as the Faroe Islands and Holland compete in often gruelling conditions for a variety of trophies.

The Newquay Rowing Club was responsible for the postwar revival of gig rowing. It purchased some dilapidated gigs from the Isles of Scilly, and later lent two of them, the *Shah* and the *Bonnet*, back to the islands for use in local races. From then on more new gigs were built. The oldest gig still racing is the *Newquay*, which was built in 1812 and is said to be the oldest wooden boat in use on the sea. The oldest gig in this neck of the woods is the *Bonnet*, built in 1830.

Gigs were often used in smuggling operations and with the option of a sail they made for very fast boats indeed. Gigs from St Ives were often rowed out to Lundy to lie in wait for the colliers delivering coal from South Wales.

The path continues behind the car park next to the Round House and Capstan Gallery and soon takes you high above the cove to Pedn-mên-du. This is a headland made up of granite that rises sharply out of the ocean. Over the years the site has played an important role as a lookout and signalling post. The concrete hut at the summit dates from around the turn of the last century, but has been unused for some years. Ring hooks cemented into the surrounding rocks were anchors for an enormous flagpole, which was used for various signals to passing ships and the lighthouse keepers.

Just inland from Pedn-mên-du lies Carn-men-ellas, meaning literally 'the rock pile stacked like sheaves'. Next to the rock pile is a cairn or barrow. It is mostly destroyed now, but five of the original stones remain in situ.

Pedn-mên-du. The hut that sits on top of this headland is a great vantage point from which to spot dolphins, basking sharks and seabirds.

The Irish Lady rock stack.

The stretch of path that runs between Sennen Cove and Land's End is probably the most trodden on the peninsula and it shows. Thousands of booted feet take their toll on the cliff tops and many smaller footpaths have been carved out, resulting in a veritable spaghetti junction of erosion. This, however, is not a modern phenomenon.

In 1935 a group of society women sold 39 acres of the Mayon Cliff to the National Trust. The group called themselves the Ferguson's Gang and were dedicated to the preservation of the countryside. They were a colourful lot, and accompanied their sales with elaborate rituals and songs. This all helped to attract the attentions of the press, which highlighted their cause. The Trust now looks after almost the entire stretch of land from Pedn-mên-du to Land's End. The footpaths are maintained and signs are put up pleading ramblers to stick to them.

The coastal scenery is particularly interesting in this region. A glance over your right shoulder gives you a good view of the Irish Lady rock stack. As you skirt Castle Zawn you get your first glimpse of Maen Castle. This well-defended cliff castle dates from around the fifth century BC (one of the earliest cliff castles in West Penwith) and is protected on the west and northern sides by sheer cliffs. The eastern side has a man-made bank and ditch defence, with the remains of a wall for added security.

If you stand within the castle you can get a great view of Land's End across the wide cove known as Gamper. Out to sea the Longships lighthouse stands resplendent in crystal waters, or shuddering under the slam of ferocious waves and howling gales, depending on how lucky you are at the time. Beyond, depending again on the weather and the angle of the sun, the outline of the Scillies can be made out, 24 miles distant. On particularly clear days you may be able to spot the white sands of the islands' many beaches. This area is truly magical, so it is well worth taking your time.

9

THE LAND'S END

Between Land's End
And Scillies Rocks
Sunk lies a land
That ocean mocks.

The lost land of Lyonesse has been incorporated into many legends, most notably those concerning King Arthur. The mythical land of milk and honey was said to stretch between Land's End and the Scillies before it was devoured by the sea. This idea is perhaps not as fantastical as it may sound. Consider the current problems we are facing concerning global warning; vast tracts of the British Isles are potentially under threat from rising seas. Could this mean that one day people will speak of a lost land of Lincolnshire?

The best evidence that Lyonesse could have existed comes from the Isles of Scilly themselves. Geological, biological and archaeological evidence clearly shows that the islands of St Mary's, Tresco, Bryher and St Martins, as well as the smaller islands, were once joined together. Old boundary walls marking field systems and village remains have been found submerged in the waters that now separate these islands, while burial chambers and stone circles can still be found on what were once the highest points on this bigger island.

A burial chamber on St Mary's, Isles of Scilly.

The Seven Stones, roughly midway between Land's End and the islands, are referred to by fisherman as the City. They are thought to mark the last remnants of the fabulous land. The Cornish name for these rocks is Lethowsow (Lyonesse). Add to that local talk of fishing nets dragging up ancient-looking cooking utensils in that area and the evidence is manifest: there was an ancient land of Lyonesse, King Arthur did rule there and Merlin flew the 50 or so miles every day to Truro to do his shopping. Anybody who says otherwise is a soulless old misery!

The great storm that finally put pay to Lyonesse is said to have occurred on 11 November 1099. An ancestor of the Trevilian family (one of the oldest in Cornwall) had foreseen what was coming and moved his cattle and family to higher ground, then West Penwith. He was returning for the rest of his

possessions when the storm blew up. He quickly mounted his horse and rode with the waves lapping at his heels, taking refuge in a cave near Perranuthnoe. A memorial once stood in the church at Sennen, erected by one Lord Goonhilly, as a thanksgiving for his own escape.

It is incredible to think that there were no lighthouses or beacons of any sort around Land's End until 1795. The number of hidden hazards, such as reefs and stacks, must have taken an enormous toll on the ships that frequented the waters in the Middle Ages; a time when England was first and foremost a seafaring nation. It must have been a time of plenty for the local communities that lived in the coastal villages who allegedly supplemented their meagre incomes from fishing, farming and tin streaming by plundering the wrecks for booty. The idea that these folk deliberately lured ships onto the rocks for such a purpose is still hotly contested, as is the notion that survivors of the wrecks were murdered to ensure there were no witnesses to the crime. It is true, however, that when petitions were sent out from ship owners and merchants to have some sort of navigational aid erected off the coast at Land's End, there was some opposition from locals fearful of losing the booty that came their way from time to time.

By 1787 Trinity House could ignore the clamour for action no longer. In 1790 they commissioned John Smeaton, he of the Eddystone lighthouse and the pier at St Ives, to carry out a survey of possible locations for a light of some sort. His investigations came up with two possible sites: the Wolf Rock and the Longships rocks. He also stated that the costs involved in erecting a lighthouse on either would be enormous. Consequently Trinity House let it be known that someone was needed to establish a lighthouse and foot the bill. Enter stage right Lieutenant Henry Smith. He realised that after an initial outlay of his own there was the potential to earn pots of cash, thanks to a clause in the contract which stated that in return for the fifty-year lease at £100 per year, he would be able to exact a levy of a penny a ton from ships passing the lighthouse. On 8 October 1791 the lease for the Longships rocks was issued, which included the option of building a lighthouse on Wolf Rock. Architect Samuel Wyatt carried out a survey of Longships and decided that the tower should be built on the larger of the rock islands and that the top of the rock would need to be removed to create a level platform. The excavated platform measured 25ft in diameter and the base of the tower was to sit neatly on it. However, before the first granite block had been put in place Smith had run out of money. He persuaded local merchants and shipping tycoons that, in their own best interests, they should finance the project. He made them a promise of a return plus considerable interest within

The Land's End Experience... take it or leave it.

Opposite: *A classic view of Land's End.*

Land's End.

four years of the lighthouse coming into operation. The money was raised and a total of 30 masons and quarrymen were employed to the task. The blocks were cut, tagged and test constructed at Sennen Cove before being shipped out to the rock. The finished tower stood over 27ft above the base rock. On 29 September 1795 the light, an Argand oil-lamp, was fired.

Over the next few years the drop in wrecking incidents in the area was substantial but Smith's creditors were getting anxious; most of them had not received a penny after their initial investment. Smith was eventually hauled before the Court of the Lord Chancery, which sent him to the notorious debtors' prison in London. He was ordered to remain there until the debts had been paid. Trinity House took over the management of the lighthouse.

Early lighthouse keepers were paid £30 a year plus food and worked alternate months. In July 1801 Robert Stevens visited the lighthouse in his capacity as engineer-in-chief for the Northern Lighthouse Board. He was shocked to see the conditions in which the keepers lived. He reported that the kitchen was being used as a rubbish tip and the Argand lamps were being used as cooking stoves, as the kitchen stove was under a pile of rotting fish. The light was so dirty that it shone red when used.

There is a famous story connected with one of the early keepers who was kidnapped by wreckers eager to prevent the lantern from being lit. They wrestled him off the rock and held him captive at a secret location in Sennen, but they had not realised that his young daughter had hidden herself away during the operation. For two days she managed to fend for herself and reportedly stacked some books on which she stood to light the lamp.

In 1836 an act of parliament gave Trinity House the powers for the compulsory purchase of all privately owned lighthouses. This affected the Longships and the family of Lieutenant Smith received the very grand total of £40 670, as there was still over nine years left on the original lease. The value of the award was based on the profits the lighthouse made in the previous years. In 1833 the clear profits stood at £3017, but by 1836 they had risen to £8293. As a footnote to the sorry tale of Lieutenant Smith, it is not known whether he ever got out of the debtors' prison, but by the time the above payment arrived the poor fellow must have died.

In August 1855 the finances were raised to build cottages at Pedn-mên-du, in which lighthouse keepers could live with their families when they were ashore. From the new cottages the keepers' wives were able to stay in contact with their husbands by using semaphore. A broad white strip was painted around the doorways of the lighthouse and cottages to make the signalling clearer. A unique mayday signal was also used if the keepers got into difficulty while on watch; an oil-soaked rag was set alight with seaweed placed on top to create a smoke signal.

The main problem with the first lighthouse on the Longships was that it was not tall enough. In rough weather the tower would disappear beneath the white surf of the crashing waves, blocking out the light from the lantern. The ships that came to grief during these periods often sank before being identified and on many occasions the first anyone knew about a disaster was when the flotsam and bodies washed up on the beach. It was clear, as shipping traffic increased around Land's End, that an upgrade of the lighthouse was required to meet demand. It was decided to erect a new tower, adjacent to the existing one. Three further sections of the rock had to be removed in order to accommodate the foundations for the larger building. The blasting left a series of steps on which the foundations would sit.

The first year of the building contract saw atrocious weather, but by 1871 the tower was completed up to the eighteenth course (the eighteenth level of granite). The foundation level was constructed in a step fashion to break up the power of the waves. By May 1872 the tower was completed to the twenty-fifth course. The weather had improved considerably in the third season and by August of that year the tower was 62 courses high. The diameter at its base was 26ft 6in. and the completed tower sits 104ft 3in. above the high-water mark. The final task was to install the internal fittings and fixtures. Operational engineers from Chance Brothers of Birmingham undertook the job, but in October 1872 a storm blew up and for six weeks the men were stranded as no ship could get near the rock to bring them to the mainland. By December they had become desperately short of provisions so a steamer was sent out in a gale. It was anchored some way off the rock and a rocket with a line, with the provisions sealed in barrels attached, was fired. However, the steamer broke anchor and almost collided with the rock. No further journeys were made until 4 January when the men were finally rescued.

The Longships lighthouse.

The lantern was installed in February 1873 but the old lighthouse still had to be dismantled. The work began but another storm blew up and the engineers watched as the old tower, with perfect timing and grace, slipped into the water after eighty-eight years of almost constant pounding from the sea. On 3 December 1873 the new lantern was officially fired. For more than a century the lighthouse has been a warning to shipping around the western tip of the peninsula. The lighthouses of Longships, the Scillies, Wolf Rock and Pendeen working in conjunction makes this stretch of coastline one of the best lit in the world. Stand anywhere along the South West Coast Path in this area on a clear night and you can marvel at the show these sentinels offer. Crosbie Garsten hits the right mood in his poem 'Sea lights':

Waves crash around the Longships lighthouse.

Flashed Lizard to Bishop
'They're rounding the fish up
Close under my cliffs where the cormorants nest
The Lugger lamps glitter
In hundreds and litter
The sea flow like spangles. What news in the west?'

Flashed he of the mitre
'The nights growing brighter
There's a mist over Annet, but all's clear at sea.
Lit up like a city
Her band playing pretty
A big liner's passing. Aye all's well with me.'

Flashed Wolf to Round Island
'Oh you upon dry land
With wild rabbits cropping the pinks at your base
You lubber, you oughter
Stand watch in salt water
With tides tearing at you and spray in your face.'

The gun of the Longships
Boomed out like a gong – 'Ships
Are bleating around me like sheep gone astray
There's fog in my channel
As thick as grey flannel
Boom – rumble – I'm busy excuse me I pray.'

They winked at each other
As brother to brother
These red lights and white lights, the summer night through
And steered the stray tramps out
Till dawn snuffed their lamps out
And stained the sea meadows all purple and blue.

10

UNDER THE WOLF'S GAZE

The stretch of path between Land's End and Gwennap Head is simply stunning. Not many venture beyond the 'theme park' so chances are you will have the coast to yourself for a while. The first point of interest sits in the sea just beyond Greeb Zawn. The Armed Knight is a granite rock stack, beyond which is Enys Dodnan, a stack with a naturally formed arch. These two stacks are part of the same granite mass that connects the peninsula to the Longships, the Seven Stones reef and the Isles of Scilly. There are no finer examples of jointing in the granite anywhere along the path. At Pordenack Point the blocks rest on top of one another, waiting for the day when they too will fall, to be smoothed by the sea. The cubic pattern created by the jointing looks as though the coastline has been deliberately 'built' by some ancient hand to resemble the walls of a castle; it is from this idea that the term 'castellated' comes. Similar structures can be seen at Carn Lês Boel a little further along. On the southern side of Pordenack Point one of the most magnificent bays on the entire walk can be seen: Mill Bay or Nanjizal.

Below Zawn Reeth is the wonderfully named Diamond Horse Cove, so named because a particularly rich vein of quartz, when discovered, was erroneously thought to be diamonds. Quartz forms when silica-rich fluids circulate in joints after magma has cooled and hardened to granite. Over countless millennia the silica is deposited on the walls of the joints, eventually sealing them.

The caves at the back of the cove once proved very handy places to store booty. (Nowadays, however, you might find it a good place to spot seals as they tend to congregate around this area for the annual moult.) Smuggling is often considered to be the illicit importation of contraband to avoid paying duties, but its origins lie in the export of wool. To regulate the wool industry in the Middle Ages, strict controls and heavy taxes were introduced. To make collection easier for the tax officials, trade was restricted to certain ports. From this grew the art of 'owling' where farmers, particularly from East Anglia and Kent, arranged secret night crossings to markets in the Netherlands and France.

Castellated rocks at Land's End.

The caves at Diamond Horse Cove.

This activity obviously had an effect on the public purse because in 1662 the illegal export of wool was made a capital offence. In 1699 rangers known as riding officers patrolled stretches of coast that were most vulnerable to this practice.

As the industrial revolution took hold and heavy machinery was invented to work the region's mines deeper underground, huge labour forces clustered around the mines, providing a market for the contraband we most commonly associate with smuggling. The adits and shafts created by the industry provided perfect hiding places. During the Napoleonic Wars (1800–15) 'free trade' was at its height; the most commonly smuggled goods included tea, tobacco and spirits. The East India Company had a monopoly on the tea trade and stored the stuff in bonded warehouses until the duty was paid. 'Free traders' buying tea for a shilling abroad could sell it for eight times as much at home. Consequently, it is believed that almost two-thirds of all tea drunk in England at this time was smuggled; 26 per cent of that entered via Devon and Cornwall. The potential profit margins also applied to tobacco; £10 worth of tobacco bought in Amsterdam could sell for £100 in England.

Such goings-on were afoot in West Penwith but with tin rather than wool. The Duchy of Cornwall was created in 1337 by Edward I. One reason for this, some say the only reason, was so that the Crown could have the right to buy all the tin produced, at prices it thought reasonable. After refinement the tin was taken to the stannery towns, originally Totnes, Saltash, Tavistock and Plympton, and later Penzance, Helston and Truro, where the ingots were weighed and stamped. The corner snipped off the ingots, for the purpose of testing for purity, were known as coins and the purity of the tin decided what coinage dues were paid. The free traders smuggled tin out of the county by taking advantage of another Cornish export; they would bury the ingots in barrels of pilchards.

The most common vessels used in the trade were cutters as they were speedy and highly manoeuvrable with a single mast and a large sail area. They also had removable bowsprits (to enable the addition of an extra sail on the bow) to increase speed further. In a preventative measure by the authorities bowsprits were outlawed on all cutters except those used by customs officials. These men were often poorly paid and inadequately protected and, to add insult to injury, they often lived in the same communities as the people they were watching. Some, it is said, 'met with accidents,' such as Benjamin Elliot who lived in Marazion in 1748. In one year he got through four horses; one went blind, two died and his last one went mad. The customs men's low pay

Enys Dodnan and the Armed Knight.

Low tide At Nanjizal.

Pendower Coves.

and, no doubt, fears for their health, often tempted them into collaborating with the smugglers or at the very least turning a blind eye.

The prize money on the contraband they seized, however, was handsome – so much so that there was fierce competition between them and their arch rivals, the excise men – customs and excise was not made a single government department until 1909.

The excise duty was levied at the time of the Civil War to raise extra capital on goods manufactured within England (such as candles, beer, malt, salt and leather). Excise men entered inns and other places of work to check that the duty had been paid. In the early days the profits to be had from smuggling were huge and the only risks, before the authorities got their acts together, came from being bamboozled by your associates. Robert Oats was an innkeeper in St Just who, with his brother Thomas, led a gang of smugglers. James Permewan, a farmer at nearby Trevear, financed the enterprise. Peter Pridlam, out of Brixham, was the agent who crossed the sea to Brest to buy goods from the merchants Larrant & Co. The first cargo (480 tabs of brandy and 200 of gin) was brought ashore at Priest's Cove; the second included 318 tabs of brandy, playing cards, candles and honey. After this drop was made a storm wrecked the boat and the captain, a Mr Davy, was drowned. A new boat was found but, according to Peter Pridlam, the third cargo had to be landed elsewhere due to unfavourable weather. In addition, all the profits went on bribes to the authorities. It also turned out that Pridlam had not paid the merchants in full. As Oats could not go to the authorities to complain, he had no choice but to relieve Pridlam of his duties and deal with the merchants himself. A fourth and fifth cargo was landed but the sixth was intercepted by customs. Although Oats took it on the chin, the farmer James Permewan, whose money was invested in the venture, was bitterly disappointed, so he reported the operation to the authorities. The case was heard in Cornwall and Oats was found not guilty. It has since been estimated that for every £500 spent in Brest a whopping £2400 was made in Cornwall, a vast sum of money in those days.

The headland that separates Nanjizal from Pendower Coves was another promontory utilised for a cliff castle. Inland from its almost indistinguishable defensive ramparts are the open fields the occupants of the castle would have farmed. The whole area has the feel of a true wilderness, time worn and desolate. The only vegetation that is able to get a foothold here is the Cornish heath and bell heather that carpets the plateau and erupts into pinks and purples in August. The dense cover the heath provides is home to a surprising diversity of wildlife.

Pendower Coves are flanked on the southern end by Carn Barra and from this vantage point you can get a good view of the caves situated below Carn Lês Boel on the far side. During a particularly large swell the waves are squeezed into this cove, increasing their height and, if there is an offshore breeze, perfect barrels can form as a result. The presence of the caves give testament to the raw energy these waves offload onto the shore. The air in this region is heavy with salt spray as the compressed air shoots up the cliffs at the back of the coves and drifts across the heathland.

From Carn Barra you can either cut across the back of Gwennap Head and head down the valley to Porthgwarra, or pick your way across the cliff tops to the headland itself. Choose the latter and the path will take you across the top of Porth Loe, the scene of the wrecking of the *Khyber*, a grain-carrying cargo vessel, in 1905. Perched high above Porth Loe is the Gwennap Head lookout station, which was being built around the same time. Ladders from the building works were used to rescue the three crew lucky enough to survive the impacts as the ship was repeatedly dashed against the rocks. This small building still keeps an eye on what is one of the busiest shipping lanes in the world. Its upkeep is funded by the National Coastwatch Institution, a voluntary organisation set up in 1994 when two fishermen were drowned in the sea below the recently closed lookout at Bass Point (on the Lizard peninsula). The institution was set up to reopen the many lookouts that have closed over the years, with the belief that although high-tech equipment has improved safety at sea, nothing can replace the human eye. Watchkeepers, as these volunteers are known, also provide valuable up-to-the-minute sea and weather forecasts to small vessels passing through the busy shipping lane. They are happy to invite you in and show you the impressive array of equipment they have at their disposal. While you are in there be sure to make the most of a particularly powerful set of binoculars they have to inspect the lighthouse that stands 9 miles out to sea.

The lighthouse on Wolf Rock is 115ft high. At its base it measures 41ft 8in. in diameter, which is solid to 39ft and stepped to the twentieth course to disperse the force of the waves. Up to the nineteenth course the granite blocks are secured with 1ft-long gun-metal bolts. The doorway is located at the twentieth course and is surrounded by 7ft-thick walls that taper on the outer edge to 2ft just below the gallery. A total of 4506cu.ft of granite was used in its construction, giving the lighthouse a total weight of 3297 tons. When the universe implodes, this lighthouse will remain! The Wolf marks one point in a triangle of navigational references in the area; the other two being Bishop Rock on the far side of the Scillies, and the Longships.

Nanjizal.

Gwennap Head lookout station.

Although barely visible above the waves at high tide, the lighthouse stands proud of the sea by 17ft at low tide. This makes it especially treacherous to shipping; there lie many wrecks in the 34 fathoms of water around the rock. The name Wolf is said to derive from the sound the rock used to make as the air was forced through a crevice within it by the waves. The howling was in itself an adequate warning to passing ships but, so legend has it, so-called wreckers from the mainland stopped the gap with boulders in order to provide themselves with a little added income from the subsequent wrecking.

Whatever the reason, the rock suddenly stopped howling, and consequently became a serious menace to mariners. Many solutions to the problem were proposed, the first being to have a bell buoy anchored just off the rock. This was opposed by fishermen, however, on the grounds that it may scare away fish. A hair-brained scheme to blow up the rock was deemed too expensive, but the entirely rational and obvious idea to bolt to the rock a huge cast-iron statue in the shape of a wolf, that would howl when the wind blew through it, was considered an excellent proposal. The wolf was duly cast and shipped out to the rock. After four days of trying to heave the great weight onto the stack, it was decided that this was a daft idea after all and the operation was abandoned. What happened to the wolf is unknown. Thumbs were twiddled and chins were scratched for some time before someone suggested the revolutionary idea of erecting a beacon on the rock, to mark its whereabouts. In 1840 the first beacon was in place, although just six weeks later it was gone, destroyed by a particu-larly nasty storm. For a further two years nothing was done as the storm had spared the white base cone and this in itself provided some warning. Eventually an iron mast with a 5ft diameter brass globe on top was erected. Once again a storm managed to bend the mast 3ft from the vertical and in 1844 it was snapped off completely. Another mast was soon erected, but this time with cast-iron stays for added stability. This did the trick until a hurricane in 1848 washed that away too, and loosened the base to boot.

The latter half of the nineteenth century saw a vast increase in sea traffic around the rock and three particular shipwrecks caused by Wolf Rock prompted Trinity House to act in 1860. The work itself began in March 1862 with the laying of the foundations. Engineer-in-chief James Walker designed the lighthouse. His plans showed that, for greater stability, the tower would have to be built as part of the rock, rather than just sat on top of it. The plans were excepted and in July 1861 Walker visited the rock to carry out a full survey. He managed to complete the task, in spite of almost being swept to his death on a number of occasions.

During the first phase of operations James Walker died from a heart attack. He was replaced by James Douglas, whose brother William took over as resident engineer. By the end of the summer of 1863 the foundations had been set and the third season of construction began on 20 February the following year. In July 1868 the final stone was set.

To call the construction of Wolf Rock lighthouse a magnificent achievement would be something of an understatement. If you look at it when on the cliffs just south of Land's End, at high tide it appears to sit on the ocean's surface. It is hard to imagine that for five years men toiled in all weathers on that speck of land in what is considered one of the deadliest seas in the world. It is incredible that not one man was lost, although many came close.

The lighthouse has stood firm against the relentless hammering from the ocean for over a century. On 11 November 1898 a hurricane tore through the region, creating waves that overshot the tower. The keeper on duty stated later that the shock of the waves was felt within, but scarcely a tremor was noticed. In 1973 the lighthouse became the first rock-based tower to have a helipad. The rotors on the craft need to remain turning upon landing in order to maintain position once landed.

The last of the keepers left Wolf Rock on 3 June 1987; the lighthouse became fully automated the following July. The beam of light from the lighthouse is 378 000 candle power and can be seen at 23 nautical miles.

Directly below Gwennap Head lookout station is Carn Guthensbrâs. You can walk out to the headland beyond it and get a wonderful view of one of the most famous rock stacks in the area: Tol-Pedn-Penwith, or the Chair Ladder. Here local witch and mischief-maker Madge Figgy sits atop the stack and wreaks general mayhem. We shall come to her later.

The stack shows clearly the natural jointing that occurs in granite and the area is a favoured site for rock climbers. During the summer months they can be seen dangling from ropes at all angles as the raging sea crashes into the jagged rocks below them.

From Tol-Pedn-Penwith the path drops a little down the cliff, along a narrow causeway, and edges round a vast hole, created when the roof of the sea cave below collapsed. This yawning chasm does not have a protective fence around it, so great care is needed.

One thing visitors to this area cannot ignore is the constant moaning sound that comes in from the sea. It emanates from the buoy anchored about a mile offshore between Tol-Pedn-Penwith and Hella Point. It warns vessels of the dangers of straying too close to the Runnel Stone. This is a treacherous rock, made

Tol-Pedn-Penwith.

The Runnel Stone land markers.

Looking across Gwennap Head to Porthgwarra.

Opposite: *Looking up the slip at Porthgwarra. One of the man-made caves is on the right.*

even more so by the fact that its summit lies just below the surface of the sea. In 1923 the steamer *City of Westminster* hit the Runnel Stone with such force that it knocked off the top 20ft. Another line of defence against this menace can be seen on the cliffs above Porthgwarra: two cone-shaped navigation markers. The seaward one is painted red, the inland one black and white. When at sea, the trick is to keep the black-and-white marker in sight. If your view of it becomes obscured by the red marker, your ship has probably been holed and is sinking fast.

At Gwennap Head you can see all the way along the coast to Treryn Dinas near Porthcurno. During a heavy swell the sea literally bulges before your eyes as the currents coming in from the Atlantic collide with those of the Channel. Cargo vessels ploughing westward pitch and roll, whereas those heading east literally surf into port as the waves pass beneath them.

It is a short walk from the spray-washed headland to the sheltered oasis that is Porthgwarra. This small inlet was once primarily a fishing cove. The slipway was built in 1880 by the local fishermen and at its top a capstan was positioned to haul up the boats. Only the granite plinth of the capstan remains after it was removed in the 1960s when the wooden spalls showed signs of rot.

Behind the remnants of the capstan is a small cave, hollowed out by hand to serve as a place to store the many lobster-pots in use at the time. At the bottom of the slip to the left are two more caves, erroneously thought to have been carved by the sea over the years. They were in fact hand drilled by St Just miners in 1890, to allow greater access to the beach for farmers wishing to collect seaweed for fertiliser. The larger of the two was originally drilled in a figure of eight, a smaller opening above the larger. In November 1996, after a spell of particularly wet weather, the granite separating the two holes crumbled away, leaving the orifice that can be seen today. The second cave was excavated in order to allow fisherman greater access to the cove from the pathway running behind Cove Cottage.

Most of the houses in the hamlet were built between 1870 and 1900 and served as homes for the fisherman, the last of whom retired in the 1960s. As a consequence of the strong tides in the area seine-nets were cast close to the shore. The last significant catch of pilchards landed using this method was in 1916. The pilchards were then transferred to large trays in the cellars of the households and covered with salt. This was known as 'scoffing', which helped not only to keep the fish fresh, but prevent damage to the scales.

To the left-hand side of the cove, near the low-tide line, are a number of wells. These are known as 'ullies' and were dug to provide wet storage for lobsters and crabs. Spaces were left between the rocks in the lining to allow the

ebb and flow of the tide to infiltrate the wells. The animals were then placed live into the pots where they could be stored fresh until sold. Food from the sea was not the only thing consumed by the residents. At the head of the valley, on the cliff between Porth Loe and Roskestal, a fowling pool was dug, designed to attract wildfowl which was shot for the pot.

The cove's secluded location meant the residents lived, worked and died there. Eventually a horse-drawn bus service, operating out of St Just, allowed them to travel to such exotic locations as Penzance once in a while. At a cost of 2s., the journey took two hours and was the highlight of the year for many of the cove's children.

Once more tragedies at sea find their way into local legend. Hella Point is locally known as Nancy's Garden and is the location of a classic tale of forbidden love. Nancy was the daughter of a wealthy farmer; William was a sailor and formerly one of the farmer's hired hands. The farmer did not approve of the match and forbade the pair's union. As is always the case, secret trysts were arranged whenever possible. One day William was called to sea on what was to be a long commission and during a tearful farewell vows of love were made with a promise of marriage from William, upon his return. It was at Hella Point that Nancy sat, hour after hour, day after day, waiting to catch sight of her returning love. Months, then years, passed and Nancy was driven to madness by her misery. Then, during yet another sleepless night, Nancy heard tapping at her window. She opened the shutters to find William standing in the cold. 'I've come for you my love' he apparently said and took Nancy down to Porthgwarra Cove. Neither were seen again. A couple of months later news arrived at Porthgwarra of the demise of William: drowned at sea in a storm off Africa. The date given for his death was the very same as Nancy's mysterious disappearance. On a still evening, it is said that the mournful ululation's of the couple can be heard as they wander the shores of the area.

As you stand atop the cliffs between Porthgwarra and Porthcurno, spare a thought for one inhabitant of these coves who is probably sick of the wonderful views. His name is Tregeagle, the wandering Jew. This legend probably has its origins in the Middle Ages when anti-Semitism was rife in Britain. The tale goes thus:

Once upon a time in a local courtroom there stood in the dock a man accused of an unspecified crime. The man protested his innocence but the only person who could confirm his alibi was dead and he was called Tregeagle. The defendant conjured the spirit of Tregeagle in an attempt to avoid prosecution. Before an aghast court the ghost gave the testimony that assured the man his

Porth Chapel.

freedom. However, as the spirit had been torn from the safety of heaven, he was once more at the mercy of the demons he had given the slip before his death. He appealed once more for the clergy to help. After much deliberation it was decided that to keep the demons at bay Tregeagle should perform a task that would last every day until the day of Judgement; he was to empty Dozmary Pool on Bodmin Moor.

His first mission kept him busy for years. One day a great storm blew up, forcing Tregeagle to take shelter. The demons saw their chance and pounced but Tregeagle escaped in the nick of time by leaping the lake, because demons (as we all know) cannot cross water. The priest at Roche Rock set him another task: to weave a truss of sand and spin a sand rope with which to bind it. The wind and waves destroyed his work and his wails of frustration forced St Petroc to move him to the coast near Helston, where he carried sand from the beach at Berepper across the estuary of the Loe. St Petroc knew this job would take an eternity; he knew the tide would carry the sand back to Berepper (a process known as longshore drift). Then one day the demons tripped him up causing him to spill the great sack of sand into the mouth of the estuary and so damming it. (The result can still be seen today in the form of the Loe bar.) Poor Tregeagle's next task is the one he still moils over to this day: to sweep the sand from the beach at Porthcurno round Tol-Pedn-Penwith into Nanjizal. At high tide his wails and moans can still be heard above the waves as his toils are washed away by the sea.

Another interesting local resident was Madge Figgy, leader of the St Levan coven of witches. She amused herself by sitting on top of the Chair Ladder, summoning great storms in order to wreck passing ships on the rocks below. The victims could then be relieved of their possessions by her sisters.

The prey of one of Madge's storms was a Portuguese passenger ship that eventually foundered at Porth Loe. Among the dead strewn on the beach was an elegantly attired African lady, bedecked with wondrous jewels. Madge ordered that she was not to be robbed as she had a strange feeling that anyone doing so would die. That night, however, avarice got the better of old Madge Figgy and she returned to the cove, took the woman's belongings and buried her in a shallow grave above the high-water mark. Returning to her hovel Madge locked the jewels in a chest.

That night a gaseous light rose from the chest and moved along the lane and down to the cove to the point where the dead woman had lain. It waited a while then returned to the chest. This was repeated every night for three months until one evening a boat arrived at the cove. At its helm was an African

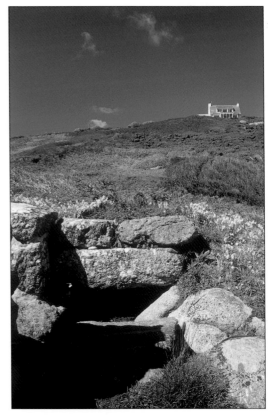

St Levan's holy well.

St Levan Church. The rock in the foreground is said to have been split by St Levan.

man who, upon seeing the light, dropped anchor and came ashore. The light led him to Madge Figgy's home and straight to the chest. He demanded that it be opened and inside he found his wife's jewels. Madge dropped to her knees and confessed all. The man asked to see his wife's grave, but as the topsoil was removed no body was there. The man and his boat had also disappeared.

The path that leads out of Porthgwarra follows the back of Carn Scathe and heads towards Carn Barges. Here you are faced with a choice: the right-hand path leads onto Carn Barges itself and down to the small but very pretty cove of Porth Chapel, while the left-hand path takes you to the tiny hamlet of St Levan and its lovely church.

Legend has it that this church was founded by St Levan after a fishing trip. He rested on the rock that sits in front of where the church now stands and split it with his fist. Whether he was annoyed at just having let go of an enormous bass, or whether he was just given to these odd outbursts of violence is unknown, but split the rock he did. He threw into the bargain the prophecy that if a packhorse with panniers could ever be ridden through the split, then the world would end. That was one cross saint! The rock, complete with its ever-widening split, sits to the right of the main doorway.

From the church it is a short walk down the valley to Porth Chapel. Above the cove sits the aforementioned saint's holy well. Like most such wells in the region it is a stone-dressed spring, built on the foundations of an earlier pagan cult of water veneration. This theme, the Christianisation of water worshipping, occurs across the region.

Porth Chapel is a lovely cove, sheltered from the prevailing westerly winds, and a favoured site for body boarders. Access to the beach is a little precarious; the path descends to a plank bridge and then leaves you to scramble down some steep rocks. The only way off the beach is via the same route. Once up on the cliff again the path gives you a steady climb up to Pedn-mên-an-mere. This small headland was where a huge radio mast was erected by the people at Porthcurno's cable operations (more of them later) to listen in on Mr Marconi's progress with his wireless. The central ground bracket for the mast is still in place, and dotted about the place are a number of smaller anchors for the supporting cables. The views from this headland are wonderful and there are plenty of nooks in which to hide should it get windy up there. You can also catch a great view of the Minack cliff-top theatre.

The path that leads off the headland takes you into the theatre's car park. This marks your entrance to one of the most beautiful coves along the entire stretch of the path: Porthcurno.

11

GIBRALTAR CALLING

The Minack theatre is named after the large rock that juts out into the ocean below it. The rock is often used by fishermen hoping to catch themselves a hefty sea bass, a fish that is fond of the white surf. During one particularly tiresome performance of a play the audience suddenly let out a raucous cheer as the fisherman they had been watching from their seats managed to land a particularly fine specimen. Everyone's a critic!

Some people say Minack should be pronounced 'Minnick' as the name originally comes from the Anglo-Saxon monastery at St Buryan. The monks and nuns called themselves Munachs and Minnchirs.

The theatre was the brainchild of Rowena Cade who lived in the large house above the theatre. In 1929 she saw a production of *A Midsummer Night's Dream* performed in the perfect setting of a shady glade, at nearby Crean. The local mover and shaker of amateur dramatics in the area was the suitably named Dorothea Valentine, a former schoolteacher who lived at the St Levan rectory, and it was she who produced the piece. Rowena Cade was inspired by what she had seen and suggested to Ms Valentine that her cliff garden would be the ideal setting for *The Tempest*.

The theatre at Minack.

The play was duly performed; the makeshift stage was a patch of lawn Rowena had cleared for the purpose. It provided some added tension as it backed onto the cliff edge. Fortunately the cast survived the play, which was met with great acclaim. From then on the construction of a permanent (and less lethal) open-air theatre became Rowena Cade's passion. She enlisted the help of Charles Thomas Angrove and her gardener Billy Rawlings for the task. They continued to make various changes to the site, as well as put on various Shakespeare productions, throughout the 1930s.

Although the site was covered in barbed wire during the Second World War and an anti-aircraft blockhouse was built above the site on Magic Rock, Rowena worked after the war to separate the theatre from her garden by a clear boundary wall. The footpath leading up from the beach at Porthcurno was added not long after, incorporating the gruelling ninety-nine steps that led to

the old pay gate. Further modifications and additions continued right through to the recent past, and all have added to the splendid cliff-top arena that is the theatre today.

The path leads off to the left of the Minack theatre and follows Ms Cade's steps down to the beach. At the top of the descent you can catch fabulous views of the cove of Porthcurno. The colour of the sea will vary depending on the time of day, weather and state of the tide. The deeper the water, the deeper the green of the ocean. When the tide recedes the green lightens to an aquamarine, as the light from the sun reflects off the golden sands beneath.

Just before you hit the beach a small path leads off to the right that takes you to the rock, much favoured by fishermen, that sits directly below the theatre. From here you can view the cove from another angle, enabling you to see right to the back of the beach. Rejoin the path that takes you over the purpose-built arch and you will be on the beach. If you are lucky enough to reach the cove at low spring tide, it will be possible to walk the entire stretch at sea level to Logan Rock. A warning for the prudish: the sheltered coves at the far side are favoured by nudists. If, however, people mincing about as nature intended doesn't bother you then this little detour is a must. Timing is paramount as the tide in this area can creep up on you, and once you are cut off from the main beach the only way is up. Although it is possible in theory to climb these cliffs, it really isn't recommended.

If you make your way up the beach towards the large car park at its rear, you will find yourself amongst the industry for which Porthcurno is most famous – the Cable & Wireless operations are located here. Just beyond the lifeguards' hut is a small concrete building that houses a multitude of ancient-looking machines used by the early operators to send signals, via the many underground and submarine cables, to the four corners of the globe. During the summer months the door to this little shed is left open, allowing you to inspect the machines up close. Further up the valley there is the opportunity to learn all about the history of Cable & Wireless at Porthcurno. Just to whet your appetite, a brief potted history will have to do for now.

Founded by local entrepreneur John Pender, the company that laid the first cable connecting Britain with Bombay, The Falmouth, Gibraltar and Malta Telegraph Company, made the cove home to the world's largest submarine telegraph station. The original site was to be Falmouth, but because of the heavy shipping around that port it was deemed too dangerous. The possibility of anchors catching the cable and so forth necessitated the move to a quieter spot, so Porthcurno was chosen. Eventually the network spread across the

Looking up the beach from Minack Point.

Opposite: *Low tide at Porthcurno.*

The heavily defended excavated caves, within which the telegraph machines were housed.

Second World War pillbox.

world. At its height Porthcurno had no less than fourteen cables operating from it. Messages were sent in 'cable code,' a type of Morse code, which was received as a wavering ink line on a piece of paper.

In 1869 the Government decided that the nationalisation of the telegraph companies would serve the empire better, so a national network was established. The terms of the buy-outs were generous so a mad rush ensued as many companies were quickly set up to lay otherwise unprofitable lines in order to cash in on the bonanza. One such cable was laid out of Zawn Reeth, between Porthcurno and Land's End, to connect the Isles of Scilly to the mainland. The steamship *Fusilier* pulled away to lay the cable which, embarrassingly, ran out before reaching St Mary's. In order to save face, the engineer in charge clamped his end of the cable tight and, full steam ahead, a dash for land was made. The cable reached, but, unknown to the admiring crowd, only because it had snapped a mile or so out under the ocean.

By 1900 Marconi was experimenting with his new-fangled 'wireless'. He had set up a station at Pen Olva on Lizard Point, and succeeded in communicating with another such station on the Isle of Wight, thus confounding his critics who had assumed that radio waves could not navigate the curvature of the earth. Soon after this some Morse code was sent from Poldhu, on the Lizard peninsula, and was heard by Marconi in Newfoundland. The Atlantic Ocean suddenly looked a lot smaller. The Eastern Cable Company erected a mast, the base of which can still be seen at Pedn-mên-an-mere, so it could listen in on Marconi's experiments. The messages suffered from static interference making them, at best, untrustworthy. By the 1920s, however, the technology was maturing. Short waves, less prone to static, were being utilised and the wireless was suddenly eating into the cable company's business. Again with the empire's best interests at heart, the Government encouraged a merger between the two competing mediums and in 1934 Cable & Wireless came into being.

Such technology and communications were a valuable target for the enemy during the two world wars; soldiers were billeted to protect the station and trenches lined with barbed wire were dug on the beach. In addition, tunnels were dug into the cliff side to house the station, with pillbox gun positions set to cover the cove. The station finally closed in 1970, by which time a training college had been established, but the legacy left by the developments at Porthcurno is manifest in today's communications-driven world.

The route that leads back to the cliff-top path is located at the back of the main beach. At the top of the steps, and to the right behind the old telegraph hut, the path takes you on a steep climb. As you reach the top you will see a Second World War pillbox that was built, along with a counterpart on the cliff across the beach, to protect the cable station.

Follow the path for about 100yds, then fork right. This will lead you to the mysterious white pyramid, that observant souls may have spied from the beach. It was built to mark the spot where a wooden hut once stood, which housed the end of a telegraph cable laid to Brest in 1880 by C.S. Faraday. The cable linked England with America, via the transatlantic connection that ran from Brest.

The path follows the cliff edge and the temptation is strong to make the tricky descent to the white sands below. Carn Kizzie provides the perfect location for a picnic. As you sit looking out on an azure sea, you will notice a small track falling away to the left that will lead you safely to the water's edge.

Continuing on the high path, you will reach another intersection. Keep right and head towards Logan Rock. You will get your first glimpse of the great reach of the Lizard peninsula; the satellite dishes of Goonhilly will be visible on

Faraday's pyramid.

The outer defences of the cliff castle at Treryn Dinas.

Treryn Dinas.

Logan Rock.

a clear day, dead ahead. Another footpath interchange now: the left-hand track takes you to the small village of Treen, where the splendid Logan Rock pub offers cracking ale and good food; the right-hand path leads you to the outer defences of the ancient stronghold of Treryn Dinas. To enter this magnificent fortress, pass through the opening in the bank. You will cross a small rock-strewn plateau that was, no doubt, the site of the main dwellings of the settlement. The people that farmed the surrounding area would have lived here, seeking refuge within the castle in times of attack.

Walk towards the end of the headland and the wall that marks the start of the fortress proper can be clearly seen. Pass through the gateway and into the heart of the complex.

This headland, above all others in West Penwith, illustrates why such places were chosen by our ancestors. The wind-weathered pinnacles of granite provide ample shelter from the elements and on days when the wind is howling, you can sit snug in a little hollow or crevice and not a hair will ruffle on your head. Also, any attackers who managed to breach the outer defences would need eyes in the back of their heads to survive in the inner sanctums. The defenders of the castle would have been able to flit in and out of sight like spirits in the labyrinth of alley-ways during combat.

Another reason people have ventured into this ancient wonder over the years has been to get a look at the famous Logan Rock. Logan Rock is a logan-stone; a huge chunk of granite that has been weathered vertically and horizontally, to create a nodule at its base, on which the stone rocks. It is said that no matter how hard you push, or what sort of leverage you use, the stone cannot be toppled. However, early in the nineteenth century a young naval lieutenant, Hugh Colville Goldsmith, was serving on HMS *Cutter*, lying off Land's End to intercept smugglers. He had heard the legend and decided to try his strength against the rock. On 8 April 1824 he and a party of fourteen sailors came ashore to try to topple the mass. After using a variety of implements, eventually the rock gave in. Goldsmith was ordered to replace the rock at his own expense – a total of £120, lent to him by Davies Gilbert, a local magistrate.

12

INTO THE RISING SUN

The route out of Treryn Dinas is the same as the way in; passing back through the outer ramparts the path continues to the right and follows the excavated ditch before dropping down into Cripp's Cove. A small climb up the far side of the valley brings you out onto Cribba Head. This headland is blanketed in a dense furze for the most part, but on the far side the bush has been cleared to reveal a plateau of heath, making it possible to get to the edge of the headland to enjoy the fantastic views to the east. Merthen Point, Boscawen Point and the lighthouse at Tater-du can all be seen clearly. There now follows a very steep descent to Penberth Cove.

Tater–du seen from Cribba Head.

Penberth Cove.

The tiny fishing village of Penberth is still home to working fishing boats. They fish mainly for mackerel and bass, with the men using baited lines to catch their quarry. Crab- and lobster-potting is still widely practiced as well, and any buoys you see out in the ocean along this stretch, marking where the pots have been sunk, have probably been set by fishermen from this cove. Penberth also possesses some renovated pilchard cellars. Here the pilchards, caught in the now-disused seine-nets, were stored before being packed into hogsheads for shipment. The cellars are used today for repair work to the crab- and lobster-pots. The National Trust, which takes care of this area of coast, has renovated an old capstan which was used to pull the boats up the slip. The Penberth Valley, which leads inland from the cove, is covered in small meadows known as 'quillets'. In these enclosures daffodils, violets and root vegetables were grown in abundance in the earlier years of the twentieth century. Now only flowers are grown and on a much smaller scale.

The path leading out of Penberth follows the far side of the cove, then heads inland a little way to bring you to the back of Le Scathe Cove. At the bottom of the cliffs above the cove are some ancient terraced fields which are still in use. A small group of offshore rocks, known as the Gazells, mark the way to

Le Scathe Cove. The terraced fields are in the foreground.

St Loy's Cove.

the next cove: Porthguarnon. A small headland sits high between the two coves and from it you can see on the far side of Porthguarnon a pretty daunting set of steps that mark the way ahead. Porthguarnon itself has, on its eastern side, a long cliff arm which serves to catch the prevailing ocean swell from the west. The resulting effect on the waves is pretty spectacular as they are channelled into the cove with ferocious energy. The cliff at the back of the cove is rapidly being worn away, giving the cove its elongated appearance.

A number of small streams pass down the valley at the back of the cove; one culminates in a small waterfall. The path crosses these and follows the steep steps on the far side. At the top it crosses the back of a number of unnamed granite ridges from which you can get a good view of the ominously named Coffin Rock that sits on the edge of Merthen Point. Merthen is very similar to Cribba Head in appearance; it is covered in furze, which makes it difficult to explore. Below the cliff edge there is a small grassy plateau that leads to the water's edge. You can get to it by crossing the headland to the eastern edge and then taking one of the many cattle tracks down. Once down there it is possible to cross St Loy's Cove, carefully picking your way among the wave-rounded boulders, below the low cliffs.

St Loy's Cove is a very unusual stretch of coast for this region. Its long, curving profile is down to the fetch of the waves, which come in at an angle from the west. They are gradually eroding the soft head material which constitutes the shoreline. It is also a catchment area for all sorts of flotsam, from shampoo bottles and wooden pallets, to seal carcasses. A stream runs out from the woodlands at the back of the cove and flows into the sea beneath the boulder beach. On quiet days you can hear its dull roar passing beneath your feet. If you were to follow the stream back up through the woods it would eventually bring you out at Trevedran, on the main road that runs from Newlyn to Land's End. Trevedran is a tiny hamlet and plays host to reputedly one of the oldest houses in Penwith.

The path leads you out of the cove and through a dense woodland of hawthorn and alder, before rising quite sharply over Paynter's Cove and up to Boscawen Point. There are a number of springs in this area, so the path doubles up as a stream after periods of wet weather. The Boscawen Cliff crosses high above Chough Zawn and Zawn Gamper and it is at this point that a very sudden change in the rock strata occurs. Look towards the next headland of Tater-du and you could easily be on the Lizard. The rock that constitutes this headland is very similar in appearance to that on Britain's most southerly point; a grey-green slate covered in a lime-coloured lichen.

The lighthouse on Tater-du was built in 1965, the last of the lighthouses to be built around the peninsula. It was commissioned in the wake of the wrecking of the Spanish coaster, *Juan Ferrer*, on 23 October 1963. The ship ran ashore at Boscawen Point and eleven lives were lost. The tower was designed by Messrs Humphreys Ltd. Fully automated and unmanned from the beginning it was opened on 7 July by the Duke of Gloucester, who was the master of Trinity House at the time. The main light gives out three white flashes every 15 seconds, at an intensity of 300 000 candles which can be seen 13 nautical miles away. Behind the lighthouse is the quarry from which the rocks were cut to build it.

From Tater-du the path follows the Rosemodress Cliff across Tol Toft. The nature reserve, founded by Derek and Jeannie Tangye, makes for a worthwhile detour. During the 1940s Derek Tangye was a Fleet Street journalist and travel-book author. His wife Jeannie was a PR officer for the Savoy Hotel. The couple were very much part of the social scene in London during the 1950s, but turned their backs on the glittering lifestyle and moved to Cornwall; they bought a rundown cottage and flower farm called Dorminack.

In 1961 Derek began a series of autobiographical books that became

Tater-du lighthouse.

The memorial cross at Lamorna Point.

A wayside cross outside Penlee House Museum and Art Gallery.

collectively known as the *Minack Chronicles*. They told of life at Dorminack, the local wildlife, and life in general around the far west of Cornwall. Jeannie provided the illustrations. She also wrote *Meet Me At The Savoy* about her days at the hotel. In 1979 the couple bought 20 acres of cliff heathland next to Dorminack and called it Oliver Land. Over the next few years they cultivated the area, which they named The Minack Chronicles Nature Reserve – A Place For Solitude. Jeannie died in 1986; Derek ten years later. They left behind some wonderfully descriptive and lively literature, as well as the beautiful nature reserve, which at the height of summer is a delight to behold. A walk through the reserve will eventually lead you onto the footpaths, which in turn lead you to the Merry Maidens stone circle.

Follow the path to Carn Barges. On top of this carn sits an unusual slab of granite that appears to have been placed on its edge deliberately. It is, in fact, a boulder that has split along a natural fracture, the front half having fallen away down the cliff, leaving what looks like a great stone plaque standing proud.

It is a short walk along the cliffs to Lamorna Point. The memorial cross you can see here marks the spot where the lifeboat men of the *Solomon Browne* lost their lives in the waters below. These men came from Mousehole and Newlyn.

In West Penwith there is an abundance of crosses, serving many different purposes. Most stand by the side of roads and trackways and are known, therefore, as wayside crosses. Their role was to mark the most direct and level routes from outlying hamlets and farms to the parish church, but some also marked the routes to places of pilgrimage such as holy wells, monasteries and priories. The tracks that the crosses stood beside were often the main thoroughfares across the peninsula and by the eighteenth century there evolved a criss-crossed network of interconnected routes.

Crosses found within churchyards often predate the church itself. They are usually oval in shape and may have been used as preaching crosses, having first been erected on spiritually important pagan sites. These are usually the oldest surviving crosses to be found and date from as early as the ninth or tenth centuries.

There follows a rather tricky descent below Carn Mellyn before the path rounds the corner and brings you into Lamorna Cove. Stretching out before you, across the cove's waters, is a long arm of granite that leads all the way up to Carn-du.

13

A NOD AND A WINK

Lamorna Cove sits at the mouth of the Lamorna valley, one of the most beautiful, and certainly the most wooded, valleys in West Penwith. The most striking thing about the cove must be the great piles of quarried granite that sit high up the cliffs on the far side as you approach. They seem ready to tumble at any minute and squash the houses that perch below them. These heaps are quarry detritus from the days when Lamorna could boast some of the finest granite in the world. The way the rock in this region jointed into almost-perfect cubes the size of bungalows made it especially desirable to the architects of large-scale building projects. Lamorna granite can be seen in many of the lighthouses in the region, and all over Britain, including the Thames embankment. One particularly huge block, measuring 22ft square, was shown at the Great Exhibition of 1851. The quay was built especially to transport the granite onto barges for dressing in Penzance.

The quarry dumps.

The cove is privately owned and kitted out with amenities; a café selling the most delicious cakes to be had along the path, as well as a gift shop with the usual tourist fare. To the back of the cove the steep road soon levels off to guide you up the valley to discover its secrets.

The first place of interest is, of course, the pub: The Lamorna Wink. The unusual name derives from the early days of the excise duty when landlords, not wanting to pay up, would hide a keg or two under the bar, to dish out when a request for a flaggon of his finest ale was accompanied by a furtive wink.

The small hamlet a little further along is nestled around a wide stretch of the stream that runs down the valley. The stream has been much changed over the years; a lot of the water was diverted for the irrigation of nearby potato fields. A small road bridge crosses the stream and leads up to an old water-mill. In the grounds around the mill wildfowl of all shapes and sizes wander freely. There are even a couple of peacocks and a peahen.

Many artists have found the wooded beauty of the valley an incentive to relocate there and devote their time to recording the many picturesque spots in and around the cove. One of the first to do so was Samuel Birch. He was born

The Lamorna water-mill.

in 1869 in Egremont near Birkenhead in Chesire. His father was a painter and decorator but died when Samuel was a boy. As a lad he worked as an office boy and at a mill near Lancaster, where he lodged with a local gamekeeper who schooled him in the ways of the country. He later worked in a linoleum factory; the labour in which he later attributed to his physical strength. During his spare time he took up drawing and soon discovered he had a natural flair for it. His mother encouraged him to widen his artistic bent and he soon moved on to painting. His pictures gradually became known locally and he made a few sales in the art gallery in Lancaster. With the proceeds, he was able to travel to Newlyn, where he had heard that a fledgling art colony was being established. He found lodgings at Borleigh Farm where he drew on the local landscape for inspiration and soon came to the notice of Stanhope Forbes, one of the founding members of the Newlyn colony. Forbes advised him, in 1895, to go to Paris and study the human form; he did just that, honing his skills at the Atelier Colorossi. He returned to Cornwall in 1902 and married a local girl. They moved to Lamorna shortly after and bought Flagstaff Cottage, the former harbour-master's house.

On the advice of Stanhope Forbes, Samuel painted under the name Lamorna to distinguish himself from another artist working out of Newlyn. His style as a romantic naturalist flourished; he worked exclusively out of doors from a small wooden studio buried deep in the woods. He had a fascination with water and was able to study it closely when partaking in his favourite pastime of fly-fishing. His early work showed little colour, but after his arrival in Cornwall his colours showed a greater intensity and his overall style brightened, no doubt as a result of the superb quality of light the county has to offer. His most well-known works are *Spring Morning* and *Tregiffian Cliff*, which lies to the north of Whitesand Bay.

Another well-known artist, Laura Knight, painted him in 1913 alongside his two children in her picture called *Lamorna Birch and Daughters*. Laura and her husband moved to Cornwall around 1905. Both being painters, they found the shifting light, changeable weather and vibrant colours a particular joy. Laura's quick brush strokes were able to catch the fleeting moments when the light fell in a certain way on a cliff or a crest of a wave. Her work between 1908 and 1912 captured the holiday mood of the place; her 1908 painting, entitled *The Beach*, attracted considerable attention at the Royal Academy. Her picture, *The Daughters of the Sun*, created a bit of a stir locally as it depicted semi-nude maidens lounging on the rocks beyond Lamorna Cove. It received many accolades from the Academy, however, and was exhibited extensively throughout the country. The couple eventually moved to Lamorna and bought a house converted from three cottages there. They also built two studios under the cliffs at Carn Barges.

Another famous artist that frequented the cove was Alfred Munnings. After arriving in Newlyn in 1910 he soon got to know a number of young students of Stanhope Forbes. He became friends with Harold and Laura Knight and even lived with them for a while before moving into the Lamorna Wink in 1911, run by a character called Mr Jory. Munnings set up a studio in the Wink's stables – an ideal location as Munnings' speciality was painting animals. His talent can be seen in the picture entitled *Lamorna Inn*, which depicts Mr Jory holding the reins to a horse as Munnings stands in the doorway of the inn. Other fine works include *Dame Laura Knight Painting* and *The Setting Sun*.

After a strained and uneasy marriage, which was brought to an end by his wife committing suicide, Munnings left Lamorna in 1917. He was sent to France as an official war artist to the Canadian Cavalry Brigade. After the war he exhibited some 47 paintings depicting the front line, with which he toured London, New York, Montreal and Toronto to much acclaim. In 1944 he became President of the Royal Academy ahead of Laura Knight and Stanhope Forbes who were also up for election that year. He died in July 1959.

As the path crosses the bridge over the stream it splits and gives you the option of either walking inland or through the quarry waste and over the top of the eastern side of the valley. The inland journey to Mousehole is a very pleasant walk through farmland, orchards and bogs (made traversable by causeways), and can be done in about half the time of the coast path. It is, however, extremely hard going if the weather has been bad. The right-hand fork in the path takes you along a tricky section of coastline, as fallen quarry stone blocks the route in one or two places, requiring some amateur athletics to bring you up to Carn-du. The headland of Carn-du offers some spectacular views in both directions; to the east the whole of Mount's Bay stretches out before you, providing your first glimpse of St Michael's Mount. Behind you the coastline you have just followed stretches back to Tater-du.

The path from Carn-du follows some stone steps down to the foot of a gently sloping, bracken-covered hillside. The trail is almost at sea level here and the shore rocks are well worth exploring. From the shore the path rises to enter the Kemyel Crease nature reserve, where Scots pines have grown to considerable heights as a result of the sheltered conditions on this stretch of coast, away from the prevailing south-westerlies.

Once out of the reserve you are subjected to a pretty exhausting time as the path winds its way across another bracken-strewn cliff side. Beneath the undergrowth lie a complex of field systems, the walls of which, here and there, show themselves, requiring you to scramble through and over them. The thick growth of vegetation in this area is down to the deep layer of head material, which provides a good soil base for roots to get a foothold. The cliff side is also well watered and on many occasions the path dissolves into a series of stepping-stones as it crosses yet another stream carrying run-off from the fields above.

The climb up to Penzer Point is made slightly easier by a few steps. At the top a bench has been thoughtfully provided so that you can rest and catch your breath. There is a small Second World War lookout post on Penzer Point, built to keep an eye on the entrance to Mount's Bay. The path from here follows a level gradient, passing by more abandoned terraced fields that lead all the way to the shore. Nearing Mousehole the undergrowth has been cleared and the open fields are used as pasture for horses. Above Point Spaniard the path joins the main road that connects Mousehole to the outlying settlements and marks the end of the coast path as a muddy, stony, rocky and precarious track. From now, until you reach St Michael's Mount, there will be only pristine, safe and less exciting tarmac, which should make life easier for those oozing blisters!

As you stand at the top of Raginnis Hill you are beginning the walk that will take you through all the major settlements of the peninsula, with the exception of St Ives. The first port of call lies at the bottom of the hill: Mousehole, 'the prettiest village in England', according to Dylan Thomas.

Looking towards Kemyel Crease nature reserve.

14

KEIGWIN'S LAST STAND

Halfway down Raginnis Hill is the Mousehole bird hospital, established in 1928 by Dorothy Yglesias and her sister Pog, a wood sculptor. Gradually the number of patients grew, so to accommodate the birds the sisters constructed wire cages at the back of their home. Neither of the sisters were ornithologists; everything they learned was through a combination of devotion to their cause and trial and error. Their skills were tested to the limit in 1967 during the *Torrey Canyon* disaster when oil-clogged birds were brought to the hospital, by this time under the direction of the RSPCA. The sisters, along with local volunteers, worked in shifts to clean the stricken animals and by the time the crisis was over an estimated 8000 creatures had been cleaned up by the team, thanks in part to nearly £4000 in public donations.

Mousehole seen from the top of Raginnis Hill.

Visiting hours for the hospital vary, but be sure to make a donation if and when you decide to pay a visit, as the hospital is run entirely on donations... and if you find a stricken bird on your travels you'll know where to take it.

Mousehole sits at the foot of a short and steep south-running valley. The source of the river that flows down it is only half a mile inland at Paul. Its course leads it under Duck Street where it emerges through a grate into the harbour. A freshwater collection point can still be seen on Treen Lane a little way from the harbour front. Water supply was never a problem in the village and that fact, along with the sheltered harbour, made the site particularly desirable to the early inhabitants. The origins of the name for the village have been lost, but it is believed to be a reference to the cave that sits to the west of the village. Alternatively it may refer to the tiny harbour entrance.

Evidence of early human activity can be found in the fields above the village, particularly to the west of the settlement. Here a number of standing stones, dating from the early Neolithic period (5000–2400BC) can be found. These are probably territorial markers connected with farming. A number of Bronze Age implements, most notably a flat-head copper axe dated at around 2500–800BC, have been discovered at the farm at Penolva, overlooking the harbour. The harbour area itself was probably not inhabited at this time.

Mousehole.

Keigwin House covers quite an area. Its frontage covered what is now the Little Keigwin, a separate dwelling next door, and the Old Standard two doors down. At the rear, in what is now known as Wesley Square, stood the courtyard, around which were undoubtedly stables and servants' quarters. The other houses in the village could have fitted into this mansion ten times over. These less grandiose dwellings, piled almost on top of each other, were centred around the harbour. A decent view was not of paramount importance to fishermen who spent their working days staring at the sea, but the way the houses were built meant that they kept each other warm. Below the homes were pilchard cellars and above them the net lofts. Stay in a B&B in the older part of the village and the chances are you will spend the night in one.

St Clement's Isle and one more of its victims.

Out beyond the harbour wall sits St Clement's Isle, so called because a chapel dedicated to the saint once stood there. Within it apparently dwelled a hermit. It is hard to see just how this fellow managed to survive as there is no freshwater supply on the island. Close inspection reveals a small patch of grass which may have sustained a cow. What can be seen on the island now is an ownership marker placed there in 1890 by Thomas Bolitho, who purchased land at Raginnis that included the island.

Sections of the harbour wall are said to date back to the Phoenicians, who were trading across Europe during the early part of the first millennium BC. If this is true then it reflects, as with the Mount, that the locals were involved in trading activity with the Continent.

Mousehole does not appear in the Domesday Book, but it probably existed and fell under the manor of Alverton, of which more later. During medieval times Mousehole grew on the back of the traditional industries, mainly fishing, to become the most important settlement in the area for a period. In 1292 the village became the first on the western side of the bay to be granted a market; it was a weekly affair, held on Tuesdays. A three-day fair and the annual fair of St Barnabas added to an already hectic social calendar. Another boon came for the village in 1383 when grants of land were made to build a quay. The presence of a decent anchorage soon encouraged wealthy merchants to settle in the village and with them came grander houses.

Mousehole, c.1860.

Merlyn Rock, to the south of Mousehole, became the site of a landing in 1595 that was to spell disaster for the village and the surrounding area. On the morning of 23 July a sea fog hung around the village, blocking out all views of the bay. Around lunch-time, as the warm summer sun evaporated the brume, it revealed four Spanish galleons anchored less than 500yds offshore. Terror swept through the village as the inhabitants watched 200 pike-welding

Keigwin House.

Keigwin House depicted in the mid-1800s.

adventurers board a number of punts and head for shore, intent on revenge for the humiliation of the Armada only seven years before. They put the village to the torch and plundered what they could. A prime target was the wealthy Keigwin House. The inhabitant, Martin Keigwin, stood his ground against the horde but paid the price. He was killed by a ball from a musket that landed in the covered courtyard to his home. A plaque commemorating the event can be seen on the spot.

Having razed the village to the ground the Spaniards marched up the lane to Paul. They burned the ancient church of St Pol de Leon (the scorch marks of the blaze can still be seen on the central pillars within) before boarding their galleons once more to head for Newlyn. On hearing of the approaching menace the Newlyners fled and, along with the people of Mousehole and Paul, gathered on the green at Tolcarne. The Lord of the Manor at Alverton at this time was Sir Francis Godolphin and it was to him that the people looked for leadership. His first action was to alert the Elizabethan hard men, Drake and Hawkins, to their plight; he was instructed to defend Penzance at all costs and hold out until reinforcements could arrive. So off everyone marched to take up positions in Penzance's market square, where they waited for the Spanish to arrive. The speed at which the defenders of the town turned tail and ran, when the attackers eventually arrived, is legendary.

After putting Penzance to the torch the Spanish were forced to retreat back to their galleons; as in 1588, a change in the wind threatened to leave them stranded and open to English attack from the sea. All that remained of the western side of Mount's Bay were a few smouldering ashes.

Mousehole had one of the biggest fishing fleets in the region, second only to St Ives, and as time passed the harbour became inadequate for the needs of the industry. In the seventeenth century the great quay on the south side of the harbour was extended. In 1838 a small quay was built out from a point underneath the Ship Inn, but this was soon replaced by an enlargement of the northern pier, which was completed in 1870. Still the harbour was over-crowded; nets and crab- and lobster-pots hung drying on any available railing; boats were being built and repaired on the wharf; carts filled with pilchards travelled to and fro between the pier and the cellars in the village. At the industry's height a total of 60 mackerel and 40–50 pilchard boats operated out of the harbour.

There is a monument in Paul churchyard that marks the resting place of Dolly Pentreath (d.1777), who some believe was the last person to speak the Cornish language as a native. It is said that Dolly used to fool tourists by muttering a few words of Cornish in search of a tip; many wealthy visitors to Penzance heard of her story and duly coughed up. Prince Lucien Bonaparte, who studied ancient languages, approached the vicar of Paul to have the monument erected to her, bearing a lengthy inscription. The locals thought that the Prince had been fooled too. The claim that she was the last talker of old Cornish is hotly disputed; in the same churchyard lie the bones of William Bodenor who died after Dolly and apparently spoke the language fluently. Furthermore, in Zennor churchyard stands a memorial to John Davey (1812–91) and his father, also John Davey (1770–1844), who are believed to be the last Cornishmen 'to possess considerable traditional knowledge' of the Cornish language.

The ancient church of St Pol de Leon at Paul. Dolly Pentreath's memorial is to the right.

Relations between the people of Mousehole and their neighbours were often strained. For example, in 1832 the town of Newlyn (the next port of call along the path) was in the ravages of a cholera epidemic, brought about when a fisherman returning from cholera-infected Ireland distributed around the town some clothes he had bought there. The people of Mousehole decided to place their neighbours under quarantine, stopping all communication and preventing anyone from there entering Mousehole. It did the trick; a total of 91 died from the disease in Newlyn, but not one in Mousehole. A field adjoining the church in Paul was put aside to bury the dead and it is still known as the cholera field to this day. However, annoyed at the enforced isolation, the people of Newlyn retaliated by banning all Mousehole people from entering their town.

Like so many of the fishing villages around the coast, Mousehole has lost loved ones in the line of work and duty. It has, however, also experienced happier times and through the people's bravery tragedy has been averted. One such tale is celebrated on 23 December every year. Known as Tom Bawcock's Eve, the celebrations remember the time when the village, on the point of starvation after rough weather had prevented the fishing fleets from sailing, was saved by Tom who braved the conditions to bring in a bumper catch. At the Ship Inn Starry Gazey Pie is served, which consists of fish, the heads of which poke through the crust to gaze at the stars. The story is retold in a beautifully illustrated book, *The Mousehole Cat*, by Antonia Barber and Nicola Bayley. Christmas sees the village illuminated by a million coloured lights and visitors flock in their thousands to wonder at them.

Another literary connection concerns Dylan Thomas and his wife Caitlin, who were regular visitors to Mousehole and frequented the Ship Inn. They were married at Penzance registry office in July 1937 and lived for a time in Newlyn. He called Raginnis Hill 'raginnis is good for you hill'.

The road out of the village follows the harbour front and joins the main coast road to Newlyn. On the way you pass the home of Cornwall's first recipient of the Victoria Cross, Joseph Trewavas. He was presented with the cross in Hyde Park in 1857; it was given to him for his services in the navy during the Crimean War, when he served on HMS *Agamemnon*. A plaque was unveiled in St Pol de Leon Church in 2002 to honour his achievements. An alternative route out of the village can be found by going through the harbour car park and past the rocky shore known as Tavis Vor. The rocks are the final resting place of a cable ship that got into trouble after losing its engines in 1999. Beyond this a wall allows you to wander along to Penlee Point, but the way back to the coast road involves a concrete stairwell before the wall. The path joins the recently widened pedestrian-cum-cycle path, past the old Penolva Quarry, now a caravan site, and heads towards Penlee Point where the old lifeboat station is situated.

Mousehole's Christmas lights.

The harbour wall takes the full force of the sea.

Mount's Bay can boast the first lifeboat in Cornwall. She arrived in 1807 but was unfortunately never used and was finally seized for debt and sold for 20 guineas in 1812. The reason for its unemployment was probably because the seamen usually called upon to effect rescue preferred to use their own tried-and-tested craft; they were suspicious of the new-fangled design of the lifeboat.

In 1826 a local branch of the newly-formed National Institution for the Preservation of Life from Shipwreck was created and a lifeboat of the Plenty class duly arrived. In 1853 a Teak-class lifeboat was delivered and housed in the first purpose-built boat-house next to the railway station in Penzance. The location was changed, however, as there were problems launching the boat against the predominantly onshore winds in Mount's Bay. By 1885 the boat-house had been moved to Penzance's quay and played host to a new lifeboat; the *Tora*. In 1895 this boat was replaced by the 12-oared *Elizabeth & Blanche*. The boat-house was moved again in 1908 when it was transferred to Newlyn. A second boat, *The Cape of Good Hope*, arrived in Penzance the following year. The boat-house that now occupies the present position was completed in 1913; the *Elizabeth & Blanche* was its first occupant. Then in 1922 the first motorised boat, *The Brothers*, arrived.

Then came one of the most fondly remembered of the local lifeboats; the *Winifred Alice Coode & Sidney Webb*, or *W&S* for short. She had an illustrious career and saw plenty of action throughout the war years. In 1947 HMS *Warspite* was being towed through the region's waters, on its way to being scrapped on the Clyde. The *Warspite* had a reputation as a ship with a mind of its own; she once broke free from the tow during a south-westerly gale, and ran aground in Prussia Cove, near Cudden Point. Edwin Madron was on his first duty as coxswain when the *W&S* was launched in a severe westerly gale. The skeleton crew on board the *Warspite* had earlier been warned of their worsening predicament and had been advised to abandon ship. The master was unable to give the command as he thought the conditions had deteriorated to such an extent that boarding the lifeboat would be suicide. The *W&S* held off and could only watch as the ship ran aground. Edwin Madron began a second rescue attempt; the lifeboat manoeuvred between the rocks and the *Warspite*, and in a swell of 30ft managed to get two lines onboard. Then in an incredible piece of seamanship the *W&S* was jockeyed back and forth in a counter motion of the waves that buffeted the two vessels. All the crew managed to jump onboard in an operation that lasted half an hour. The wreck of the *Warspite* remained on the rocks for some time afterwards and provided an interesting spectacle.

The footpath continues past the site of Newlyn's old battery. These gun positions were built in the late-eighteenth century to blow holes in Napoleon's forces, should the decision have been taken to invade Britain. Not much remains of the complex as the area is now the site of the Penlee Quarry, now disused. The works produced a very hard rock known as basaltic magma. Its strength made it desirable for use in concrete, and the blocks were even used to build bank vaults. If there is time, a path across the road at this point will eventually bring you out onto the cliffs above the quarry. From there you can get a great view of the place, now used as a freshwater refuge for all manner of seabirds.

Penlee Quarry today.

15

COSMOPOLITAN MOUNT'S BAY

To the right as you enter Newlyn is a recently built set of cottages called Rosebud Court. On a plaque outside the wall of the complex is a small wooden section of hull that once belonged to the *Rosebud*. This trawler took centre stage in a famous protest organised by the people of Newlyn against developments under the 1936 Housing Act. This act would have seen many dwellings subject to the powers of compulsory purchase and bulldozed to make way for new housing. The people of the town, horrified at this proposal, knew that the signing of petitions alone would not sway the Minister of Housing. They needed a high-profile demonstration that would alert the other MPs in Westminster to their plight; on 19 October 1937 they sailed the *Rosebud* from the harbour along the South Coast and up the Thames to deliver the petition by hand to Westminster. The stunt was a triumph; the plans, although not completely scrapped, were heavily modified, safeguarding the buildings closest to the harbour.

A section of the Rosebud, *now part of a plaque.*

During the Second World War the *Rosebud* served as a patrol ship before returning to her role as a fishing boat, although she was renamed the *Cynthia Yvonne*. She was purchased in the 1970s by a Mr Woolley who planned to take her on an expedition to raise the *Titanic* but instead she ended up a rotting hulk on the sands at Hayle. All that remains of her you can see on the plaque.

The town of Newlyn evolved from a number of small hamlets that were situated around this sheltered corner of Mount's Bay. Off the coast, between Newlyn and Mousehole, is a deep-water anchorage site known as Gwavas Lake. The area was a convenient shelter out of the brisk south-westerly gales.

Newlyn was granted its charter in 1337 and paid an annual duty to the Duchy of Cornwall, which was based on the number of boats operating from it. The sum around that time was only 10s., indicating that the town was yet to gain the importance it has as a fishing port today. Mousehole, the Newlyn of its day, paid £5 in the same year, while Marazion paid £2. By the seventeenth century the parish of Paul, which included Newlyn, was the most important centre for fishing in the county and a flourishing export industry, mainly in pilchards, had developed. The main consumers were the predominantly Catholic countries of France, Spain and Italy who ate the oily fish on Fridays. Exports have been recorded as early as the sixteenth century.

Another financial burden on villages and towns in Cornwall was the tithe system. This was a tax levied by the Church for its upkeep. Many tithes were subsequently taken over by private landowners whose lands fell within a particular parish; much of the money was not spent within the Church, which caused consternation amongst the already poor subscribers. William Gwavas inherited the rectory at Paul in 1669 and as a result, benefited from the tithes. In 1725 there was open revolt amongst the fishing community of Newlyn, who refused to pay. It seems 118 fisherman were sued by Gwavas for the non-payment and the court found in his favour. One morning in 1830 the bailiff was in Mousehole to collect the tithes when he was set upon by the women of the village. It had been a poor season and money was particularly tight that year. As the baillif retreated he made the mistake of going via Newlyn where he was attacked again. No further tithes were collected after that.

For many years the pilchard harvest was the primary money earner for the port. The only problem was that they were illusive fish; their habits were inconsistent, making them difficult to catch. In the southern oceans of Britain they usually spawn in the entrance to the Channel, nearing the shores of Cornwall in summer, but the time and place of these approaches vary year on year. Nowadays sonar is used to detect the shoals but before this the most productive method was with the use of drift nets and huers (men who stood on the shore looking for the fish). Another way of spotting them was with men in support boats called lurkers. The main seine boats were usually between 30ft and 40ft long, low sided with a broad beam and sharp bows. It took eight oarsmen to propel these boats, at considerable speed, through the water. A third boat, known as a volyer, carried the tack net, which dredged the bigger seine-net for any fish caught. The volyer then transported them back to port. Drift fishing involved larger boats called luggers, which were after a different quarry: mackerel.

The height of the mackerel season was between March and July, and towards its end the bigger luggers would sail to Ireland to take part in the summer herring fishery. They then continued up the west coast to Scotland, pursuing the herring through the Caledonian Canal to the east coast. This meant that the fisherman were sometimes away from their families for months on end.

Early in the twentieth century, however, shoals of herring were discovered off Plymouth and this season lasted through the winter, bringing the boats

Opposite: The harbourage at Newlyn.

Newlyn foreshore today.

back to Newlyn again, ready for the start of the mackerel season. No rest for the fisherman.

Line fishing was traditionally used to catch the bottom-feeding fish (cod, haddock, sole and turbot) but in the eighteenth century the trawl method began to supersede the hook and line. The very nature of this system (weighting a net, casting it, then trawling it along the seabed) meant that bigger ships were needed in order to pull the trawl. The gradual introduction of steam power soon provided the force without the need for a large boat, but the Cornish fishermen were initially reluctant to convert because coal had to be imported from South Wales, which was a costly business.

On the wall of the Smuggler's restaurant on Fore Street you will see a plaque, commemorating one of Newlyn's most famous sons: William Lovett. The Methodist chapel, on Church Street, now stands on the site of the thatched cottage in which he was born, on 8 May 1800. A trained cabinet-maker, Lovett was always looking for opportunities to improve his education, involving himself in social, scientific and political societies. Within these clubs he met others who shared his growing awareness of the pretty deplorable social and working conditions of the lower classes. Lovett was a firm believer that education and temperance led the way to social reform, and advocated reason rather than force to achieve these ends. In 1831 he refused to join the militia arguing that, as he did not have the vote, he did not feel obliged to take up arms to protect the rights and property of others when his own rights were not recognised. For this stand he was fined and his goods seized. The population of Britain was 25 million at this time yet only 800 000 were eligible to vote. Lovett exposed the conditions in the workhouses and wrote a document known as the People's Charter in an attempt to improve things. He was a member of the Grand National Consolidated Trades Union. At a meeting in Birmingham in 1839, Lovett was arrested for speaking out against the violence used by the police. He was imprisoned for a year in Warwick Gaol as a result. Whilst in prison the irrepressible Lovett wrote the book, *Chartism, or a New Organisation of the People*. He died aged seventy-seven but the benefits of his legacy are still felt today.

It was clear that Methodism and its doctrine had had a profound effect on Lovett. Methodism's founder, John Wesley, visited Newlyn fourteen times between 1747 and 1789; in 1748 he referred to the Newlyn congregation as 'a rude, gaping, staring rabble rout'!

Newlyn has a reputation as a honey-pot for artists. Those that arrived in the 1880s were distinguished by their youth and their adherence to the 'en plein air' style of painting. Many studied with, or had been influenced by, the French Jules Bastien-Lepage (1848–84) who believed that Realist artists should paint subjects in their natural settings. He felt that artists should not seek to expose the social conditions of their subjects – that was the work of philanthropists and politicians – but merely to record them and let the virtue of the people and their environment speak for itself.

The first of the recognised artists were Walter Langley and Edwin Harris, but it was the arrival of Stanhope Forbes that gained Newlyn national and international recognition as an artistic centre. He arrived in Newlyn, from Brittany, in January 1884 after searching the Cornish coast for a suitable venue to use as a base. He had walked to Porthleven and Helston looking for possible spots and wrote to his mother, 'Newlyn is a sort of English Concameau and is the home of a great many painters'. Models were apparently readily available: '... the girls are pretty, despite their rather ugly English costume, they charge six pence an hour'.

Shortly after his arrival Forbes began work on the painting that would set the ball rolling for him and the colony. The work began as a 9ft by 5½ft monster, rather clumsily titled *The Arrival of the Boats with the Fish and the People Standing Around on Wet Sand*. After many alterations, smaller studies, additions and considerable time (it took him from June to the following January to complete) the picture was finished, by now measuring only 5ft by 4ft and with the neater title of *Fish sale on Newlyn Beach*. It caused something of a sensation. Norman Garstin described it thus: 'The fresh vitality of it seemed like a wholesome breeze from the sea, breathed into a studio reeking of oils and turpentine, while its brilliant new technique fell upon the younger painters as a revelation.'

Forbes was seen as an innovator and his leadership was recognised in the community. Forbes' style (literally painting in the open) was considered the result of a visceral desire to work directly from nature and the human figure in its everyday environment. 'Nature is hard to beat' enthused Forbes. 'I advise you to approach [her] with a reverence and take what she gives you and be contented.'

Other fine painters were already living in Newlyn when Forbes arrived. Walter Langley and Edwin Harris were probably the most eminent, but those that followed began to change the direction of English painting for good. Other artists new to the scene included Ralph Todd, Leghe Suthers, Frank Bramley, Henry Tuke and Norman Garstin. Many shared lodgings with Forbes, who lived at Bellvue up Chywoone Hill.

Not all artists fitted in well in Newlyn. Henry Detmold was at first welcomed into the fold by Stanhope Forbes who saw him as a 'clever painter' but his opinion changed on further acquaintance. Detmold also fell out with many of the other artists, and got into deeper trouble with Forbes in 1886 when he became a rival for the affections of a Miss Armstrong, who became Mrs Forbes in 1889. Later in the year Forbes was irritated to see one of Detmold's paintings, already twice rejected, hanging in the Royal Academy. Detmold was nevertheless a talented artist and his works *Departure of the Fishing Fleet* (1889) and *Spearing* (1892) were particularly well received.

By the late 1880s works from the Newlyn colony were regularly exhibited in London. The reputation of the artists in Newlyn was good and their social lives were lively; few lodging-houses were without a piano and regular soirées were held around them in the winter months. In the summertime charabanc outings were taken to Lamorna and St Ives to visit other artists and a healthy exchange of ideas and techniques took place.

Two other painters of note who spent time in Newlyn were Henry Tuke and Thomas Gotch. Tuke made his first visit to Newlyn in 1883. Gotch was one of the first artists in Newlyn and was influenced by Forbes and his 'en plein air' techniques (particularly notable in his 1891 painting *Sharing Fish*). His wife, Caroline, was also a fine painter. She used to capture her subjects first on camera and then paint from the prints. Her 1891 work, *In the midst of death we are life*, was done this way.

Walter Langley depicted the more tragic aspects of the Cornish fishing way of life. Before 1890 he mainly painted with watercolours, but with his switch to oils came his depiction of heart-rending scenes. His work, *Never morning wore to evening but some heart did break*, lines from the Tennyson poem 'In Memorandum', shows a young wife sitting with her mother, mourning the loss of a loved one at sea. The painting made a considerable impact on the Academy which led to an offer of purchase by the Chantry Bequest. The painting had already been sold, however, and the new owner refused to sell it back, even at a considerably inflated price. Another of Langley's paintings worth mentioning is *The Orphan* (1889) in which two fishwives look on sympathetically as a young waif tucks into a bowl of gruel.

Newlyn began to expand as a town quite rapidly after alterations to the harbour in the early 1890s. The increased traffic brought with it a greater prosperity. New houses were built on the hills above the old town. Forbes noted that because of this the town began to lose a little of its former charm. Purpose-built studios were also developed, many at the bottom of a lane known by the artists as Rues des Beaux Arts. A field here was bought by a member of the arts group called Arthur Bateman. On the land he built a studio for Stanhope Forbes and Frank Bramley. As more studios sprang up on the site it became the place where the artists' works were displayed before an invited audience prior to exhibition at the Royal Academy.

The art gallery in Newlyn opened in October 1895. The money for its construction was donated by John Passmore Edwards, a newspaper profiteer and one of the great nineteenth-century philanthropists. Newlyn had the first purpose-built art gallery in the country. It was not designed to be a museum but a living showcase for contemporary artists. Dedicated to the first of the Cornish artists, John Opie, to this day it exhibits some of the most innovative works the region has to offer.

Newlyn Art Gallery.

The artists contributed to the life of the village in other ways too. The Newlyn Industrial Class was founded in 1890. This venture was aimed at providing employment during bad fishing times. A local benefactor, T.B. Bolitho, provided the initial funding and, along with J.D. MacKenzie's expertise, the class started producing fine pieces of copper work. John Pearson, a metal beater and founder of the Guild of Handicraft, later joined the class which went on to produce a wide range of domestic and decorative items. One particularly splendid piece of copperware can be seen on top of the National Mission to Deep Sea Fishermen. The galleon on the clock tower was made by Tom Batten and Francis Clemens. There were also classes in enamelling and silver work, held by Reginald Dick, whose wife also taught embroidery. In 1920 the Cryséde silk works was established by Alec Walker. The material was sold by the yard or made into garments designed by his wife, Kay Walker.

Past the fish market on the right stands the National Mission to Deep Sea Fishermen. This institute was established in 1881 to spread the word of Christ (and cheap tobacco) to fishermen working the North Sea. The building was initially called The Stanley Institute at the request of a Mrs Parker who donated £500 so that the mission would be named after her late father. In 1904 Miss Nora Bolitho visited the mission on a number of occasions to read to the fisherman from novels and newspapers. She donated £3000 towards the building of larger premises, dedicated to her sister Mary Foster. The building that stands today was opened on 30 September 1911 and the mission still administers to the needs of the people who work the nearby harbours.

National Mission to Deep Sea Fishermen.

Between Newlyn and Penzance the path follows the Wherry Town foreshore, past the memorial gardens built in the wake of the First World War, and the well-used bowling green, before merging with the huge promenade that takes you all the way to the harbour area in Penzance. Although this stretch of coast appears to be rather featureless, it is well utilised by the locals, particularly during the town's fish festival and annual raft race.

A little further along the foreshore, and just over 160ft from the shoreline itself, a reef is exposed at low tide. In 1778 Thomas Curtis, a miner from Breage, decided to invest his money in sinking a shaft into the reef in an attempt to extract tin. Although everybody told him he was mad to try it, he nevertheless went ahead and against all the odds he extracted some tin ore. He died in 1791 before he made his fortune. Realising that he had been on to a good thing others continued to work the mine; a total of £70 000 worth of tin had been extracted by the time a ship, which had broken anchor, drifted into the mine and completely destroyed it in 1798.

The next stretch of the Penzance foreshore is well used by local youths as a meeting and general 'hang out' area. A group of local residents clubbed together, funded and built a skate park for them to use. It seems to have worked a treat, as calls of 'see you down the skate park at seven' reverberate around the maths lessons at the local schools.

The promenade stretches for a considerable distance along the Penzance foreshore and eventually comes to an end at Battery Rocks, where the outdoor swimming pool is situated. From here you can take any of the roads on the left, which will bring you into the major town on the peninsula: Penzance.

The site of Wherry Mine today.

16

HOLY HEADLAND

Penzance lies 280 miles west of London and 10 miles east of Land's End. Its name derives from Pensans, meaning 'holy headland'. The headland in question is the southern termination of a ridge that stretches across the peninsula from Bosigran Castle on the cliffs at Zennor. The rocky outcrop stretches south-east into Mount's Bay and the headland was considered holy because of a chapel, probably Celtic, that was situated there. A little later another chapel was built further inland, standing on the spot where the present church now stands. The outcrop provided shelter from the prevailing winds and from this vantage point a hamlet grew.

The earliest evidence of human habitation comes in the form of stone axe heads found in excavations around the area. Analysis has proved that these

Approaching Penzance.

The extensive harbourage at Penzance.

were made from a rock known as The Gear that now lies submerged half a mile offshore. At the time these axe heads were fashioned, a vast swathe of forest covered what is now Mount's Bay; at extremely low tides, and after rough weather, remnants of this wood can be seen poking out of the sand in the shape of tree stumps and logs. The Gear rock, along with the Mount itself, would have sat among the trees, serving as quarry stone for these early inhabitants.

Bronze Age arrowheads, as well as storage and cooking jars, have also been found. These belonged, no doubt, to the inhabitants of Lescudjack Castle which sat high above the bay on the promontory that is now skirted by the A30 bypass. The only remains of the castle are a series of defensive earthworks (although these date from the Iron Age).

Signs of Roman occupation this far west are minimal, although two coins bearing the name of the emperor Vespasian (AD69–79) have been found in the cemetery of the church. As has been mentioned earlier, European trade in tin was well established by the time of the Roman period. Most of the export activity was centred around the Mount and the Romans seemed happy enough to leave it at that. The nearest indigenous settlement of any note dating from this period is at Chysauster, 2 miles to the north of Penzance. The remains of this ancient village, home to a farming community, are well preserved.

In AD930 Athelstan annexed Cornwall and founded a college of priests at St Buryan on the site of an earlier Celtic settlement. The sphere of Saxon influence only really affected the Cornish in the north-east of the county around the Tamar; a quick look at the map of West Penwith and it becomes apparent that virtually all the settlements have Celtic names. There is one important exception, however; Alverton is a suburb lying to the west of Penzance and was first recorded as the manor under whose jurisdiction Pensans fell. The name Alverton originates from Alwarton, referred to as 'the important settlement of Alwar', who may have been a Saxon thane. Alwar (it was retrospectively recorded in 1284) was relieved of his lands by Robert, Count of Mortain, half-brother of William the Conqueror. The lordship of Alverton remained in the hands of the Duchy of Cornwall until 1230 when the then duke, Richard, younger brother of Henry II, granted the manor to Henry le Tyes. It remained in his family until 1322 when the incumbent at the time, Henry Lord Tyes, took part in one of the many rebellions against Edward II. The King, in one of his more dynamic moods, executed him and took his lands. In 1327 the lands were restored to Henry's sister. In 1466 the manor was once more forfeited to the Crown and Henry VIII was the Lord of Alverton Manor when the Harbour Charter was granted in 1512.

There was always fierce competition for trade between Marazion and Penzance; the Mount at Marazion had long had a harbour at which vessels could dock at high tide. Traders could then either reach the town by row boat, or on foot when the tide was low. Penzance suffered a blow in this competition when Marazion was given its Charter of Incorporation in 1595 by Elizabeth I.

Such charters were important as they gave a town independence from the rural administration of the county and provided the legal and constitutional framework for the town to administer its own affairs. From 1595 it seemed that Marazion was destined to be the major town in the bay, but a charter was granted to Penzance in 1614 by James I and the balance of power once more tipped in favour of the town. A common seal was quickly adopted which was, rather comically, St John the Baptist's head on a charger. Holy Head... get it?

Pirates were a common problem to the trading vessels entering the waters off Cornwall at this time. The main protagonists of this way of life were Moors from North Africa, commonly called Turks. They harried the traders to such an extent that by 1625 it was beginning to affect the import trade in Penzance. Roger Polingbroke felt obliged to petition the Government on this matter, asking for eight pieces of ordinance and a £600 grant in order to build fortifications. In 1640 it was reported that, in sight of the town, four Turkish ships had captured five Penzance fishing boats and four trading ships. Shortly afterwards things took a turn for the worse; some Turks actually landed in the town and made off with 60 people.

Penzance, from an old print.

After Cromwell's triumph, local Royalists, Thomas Gross of St Buryan, William Keigwin of Mousehole and Captains Maddern of Penzance and Tresillian of St Levant, answered the call from Sir John Arundell of Trerice and rebelled on 16 May 1648. Arundell was the defender of Pendennis Castle at Falmouth and held out for five months after the rest of the Royalist forces had surrendered at Tresillian Bridge near Truro on 12 March 1646.

During the Civil War Penzance, like most other towns in England, was home to both Royalist and Parliamentary factions. The war in Cornwall lasted from 1642 to 1646, and Penzance was a staunch Royalist town. There was not much action of note during the conflict itself, primarily due to the fact that the Lord of Alverton Manor at the time was one Alexander Daniell who, although a Royalist at heart, prudently took no side in the discord. There was, however, a Royalist uprising in 1648. By 22 May Parliament had summoned enough troops to attempt to retake the town, and under the command of Sheriff Edward Hark and Colonel Robert Bennet they did just that. The uprising finally ended on 23 May.

The Jubilee Pool on Battery Rocks.

Plague struck the town in 1647. The parish register shows that the number of burials rose from 30 in 1646 to 150 in 1647; July was the worst month with 64 burials. Despite all this, the town received a boost on 8 August 1663 when it was granted its coinage charter. The period of the Restoration saw Cornwall viewed with favour by a king recognising its Royalist stance. Perhaps the charter was Penzance's little kickback because prior to this all the tin was exported from Gweek on the eastern seaboard of the Lizard, due to the fact that nearby Helston was the only stannery town in the area. The charter was granted after much complaint from miners in the St Just region who argued, quite reasonably, that the considerable trek to Helston was costing them dearly, in both time and money. As a result of the charter the position of Penzance as the major commercial and civic centre in West Penwith was guaranteed, and there was nothing Marazion could do about it.

The promenade terminates at the Jubilee Pool; a wonderful outdoor swimming pool built in 1935, in the art-deco style. You may hear the locals refer to this site as the Battery Rocks; in 1740 a battery was built there as war with France seemed imminent. Fearing for the exposed position of the town and the possibility of it being attacked from the sea by the French, a petition was made to the Government for 'great guns' to safeguard against such an eventuality. The Government agreed, on the condition that the town stump up the cost of building the battery in which the guns would be housed. The 1740 accounts show that £200 was spent on labour and materials such as stone, clay and lime. By November of that year the battery was completed and the guns put in place. Still the townsfolk were uneasy; there was always the possibility that the guns could miss their target. As a result an independent company of volunteers was raised by George Borlase, armed with muskets and other weapons taken from the wreck of the *Charming Molly* that had recently run aground offshore. In 1756 the volunteers were mustered for action when a French privateer attempted to raid the town. They could only watch from the shore, however, when winds kept his ship, complete with 22 9lb guns and 280 men, at bay.

In 1800 the Napoleonic Wars broke out, and lasted intermittently for 15 years. Business for the town was swift during these times; cargoes were shipped in and out of port on their way to and from the Continent. The death of Nelson at Trafalgar is said to have been announced in Penzance before anywhere else. The story goes that the schooner *Pickle* was carrying the dispatch to Falmouth when it passed a Penzance fishing boat off the Lizard. The news was conveyed to the fisherman who duly returned to port with the intelligence. The mayor, Thomas Giddy, was hosting a ball in the town's assembly rooms, now the main dining-room of the Union Hotel, and was the first to receive the news. It must have been his finest hour when he hushed down the proceedings to relay the bombshell.

However, this glory was short-lived as Penzance was probably the last to hear of Wellington's victory at Waterloo. The borough accounts for 1815 show a payment was made to the gunners at the battery to fire the cannons in salute at the triumph on 29 June; Wellington was victorious on 18 June. A few weeks later 'Old Boney' got his first and last glimpse of Cornwall as his prison ship *The Bellerophon* rounded the Lizard on its way to anchor off Plymouth Sound, before heading for St Helena.

From the Jubilee Pool the promenade joins Wharf Road, and brings you into the heart of the town's dry and wet dock areas. On the left is the Trinity House National Lighthouse Centre, converted from the old headquarters built during the operation to construct the Wolf Rock lighthouse. On the right the wet docks can be found; this area harbours all manner of ships, and over the road is the old weighbridge for vehicles transporting cargoes to and from them. The south pier is the embarkation point for passengers boarding the *Scillonian* bound for the Scillies. The dry docks are on the left beyond the museum; the bridge spanning the harbour is raised to let boats into this dock for refits and maintenance. The *Scillonian* is a regular visitor during the off season.

As you cross the bridge a look up to the right will reveal the back of the buildings that run along Chapel Street. Beyond the bridge on the right is the marina, home to a flotilla of pleasure craft of all shapes and sizes during the summer months. Next to the marina, the extensive car park is well used by locals and visitors alike as they make the most of the multitude of shops Penzance has to offer. The way to the main shopping streets is via the Wharfside shopping centre, which now dominates the vista. The bus and train terminals are conveniently located next to each other at the end of Wharf Road and it is from there that you can explore the peninsula and beyond very cheaply.

The first railway to be built in Cornwall was in 1837, between Hayle and Redruth, and was operated by the West Cornwall Railway Company. The route was originally a mineral line and did not carry passengers until 1843. In 1852 the line between Penzance and Truro was opened after much delay. The line provided the people of Penzance with a cheap means of getting beyond their usual boundaries. However, Penzance was not yet connected directly to London and the main network; the quickest way of getting to the capital was by train to Hayle then steamer to Bristol, followed by another train to London.

Chapel Street. This road plays host to some of the oldest buildings in the town. As well as the Union Hotel there are the Admiral Benbow and Turks Head pubs; the former may have been the setting for the opening chapters of Treasure Island *(Jim Hawkins' father ran the inn). However, opinion is split – many people believe that the inn in question was actually on the Devon coast. The mother of the Brontë sisters lived in a fine Georgian cottage further along the street.*

The old lighthouse depot.

On 2 May 1857 Brunel opened his famous bridge across the Tamar, and the rail link at Saltash made the all-important connection. West Cornwall had lost its isolation for good – whether this was for the better is still a matter of conjecture! In 1866 the Great Western Railway bought the West Cornwall Railway and the line to Penzance was converted to wide gauge. In 1892, however, the entire network was transferred to the small gauge we all know and love today. The station that marks the terminus to the line was built in 1881. At the time the approach viaduct stood only 12ft above the sea. On many occasions this stretch was damaged during stormy weather so in 1891 it was rebuilt and heightened, with the stone causeway reinforcement completed in 1921. The commercial opportunities the railway offered the town were enormous as Cornish fruit and vegetables were sold at London markets. In addition, matters of civic importance could be put to parliament far quicker than before.

The nineteenth century saw Penzance really come into its own; in 1801 the population of the town stood at 3382, but by 1871 it was 10 425. All of the civic buildings standing today were built in the nineteenth century; the domed market house, the geological museum, the tidal and floating docks, the dry dock, the promenade and Wharf Road all shaped Penzance.

By the 1880s communications were better than ever and industry was everywhere. The town was producing, for export and local consumption, many important items that before – and sadly today – had to be imported. There was tin smelting by Messrs Bolitho & Son at Chyandour, while Gulval had an ice works, an aerated-water factory for soft drinks and a flour mill. Rope makers served the miners and fishermen. Chyandour, Penzance and Heamoor saw basket makers working all hours supplying crabbers and other traders. Newtown near Marazion had one of the largest brick manufacturers in the South West. Lariggan had a flour mill, Towednack and Tredinney were home to china-clay workings and there were boat builders galore. Stone quarrying took place at Penlee, Sheffield, Newmill, Lamorna and Castallack. Penzance had a gasworks as well as an iron foundry plus a sawmill in Coinagehall Street, and another at Wherry Town. There were five leather curriers in the area, plus two tanneries at Chyandour and one in Alverton. Penzance had three coach builders and four furniture makers, while Mount's Bay steam works busied itself with curing ham, sausages and hogs pudding and marinating pilchards.

The railway also brought in a new industry: tourism. Conflicts arose between the more traditional industries and this new one. For instance, the promenade had been built on the fishermen's traditional net-drying grounds and so holiday-makers complained that the fishermen, when bringing their boats onto the beach to dry their nets, obscured the view from the beach huts. In 1861 the Queen's Hotel was built and in 1876 the Corporation of Penzance finally took the plunge and sold the town as a holiday resort.

Censuses from 1801 showed the town to have an increasing population, which reached its height at 13 328 in 1911. The next census showed a decline and marked the beginning of an almost imperceptible deterioration in the town's fortunes. One of the major factors was the slump in the mining industry. Cornwall could no longer compete economically with the mines abroad, many of which were worked by Cornishmen, forced into emigration to look for work. All over the world, particularly in Australia and the central American countries, the familiar engine houses can be seen. A saying goes that wherever there is a hole in the ground, no matter where you are, you will find a Cornishman in there digging for tin.

The beginning of the First World War marked the town's 300th anniversary of the granting of the charter. To commemorate the event the gardens were laid between Newlyn Art Gallery and the Luggan river. During the war troops were billeted in the town for training proposes and a camp was set up at Chyandour for German prisoners of war. In 1915 a naval base was established which was mainly concerned with escorting convoys across to France. The 1922 memorial commemorating the dead stands on Battery Rocks by the Jubilee Pool.

In 1934 the borough was enlarged. A new coat of arms was designed, surprisingly to include a pirate. This was surprising because one of the reasons the charter was granted was for the town's services in suppressing piracy. The other features on the arms are the Lamb and Flag of Gulval, the hot mark used by the iron-smelting company, a Maltese cross for Madron (symbolic of the knights of St John), the crosses of St Andrew and St Paul (for Newlyn and Paul), the crest of a ship and the crown of St Antony (the traditional saint of Penzance). Funnily enough the arms do not include the severed head of John the Baptist on a silver platter.

Wharf Road today.

Between 1940 and 1942, a total of 16 people were killed in the town by enemy bombs and 48 houses were destroyed. The era from the Second World War to the present day has seen Penzance grow as a tourist destination. Many people use it as a base from which to explore the peninsula. The increase in car usage has created great problems over the years. Even today the town can become strangulated by traffic, as its inhabitants choke in an invisible fog of carbon monoxide. The problem reached a crisis in the late 1980s; the only way to Land's End was through the town. As a result a bypass was built. The town still comes alive in the summer months, although it never regains the bustle of the late-nineteenth century.

Way back in 1332 the first markets and fairs were granted to Penzance. These included a Wednesday fair, mainly for traders, the Corpus Christie fair and probably the most important of all, the Golowan, which was more of a festival. The name Golowan derives from Gol Jowan, old Cornish for John's Feast – the John in question being St John the Baptist. There was great revelry on these occasions; lines of dancers weaving their way through the lanes crying 'an eye, an eye' whereupon the leading two dancers would stop and hold hands above their heads in an arch to create the 'eye' through which the line would pass, until the call came up again. The highlight of this celebration was the lighting of bonfires and a torch procession through the streets of the town on midsummer's eve. A quay fair was held the following day. This festival has been revived in recent times; on the weekend nearest the summer solstice the main thoroughfare, Market Jew Street, is closed off and market stalls set up. A tent is erected on the car park across from the Jubilee Pool in which bands play and the local brew flows. All around the town, in pubs and small theatres, even on the streets, performers entertain. Local schools and societies build floats and giant effigies to take part in the parade through the town. The event is a must if you are in the area at the right time of year.

We cannot leave Penzance without a word about its most famous son, Humphry Davy. A statue of the man stands outside the old council building at the top of Market Jew Street; it is positioned here in order to be in close proximity to the house in which he was born in 1778. Throughout his career he discovered a number of chemical elements including sodium and potassium in 1807. He was knighted in 1812 and then given special dispensation from Napoleon to travel across France for a couple of years, during which time he discovered iodine. In 1815 he received an invitation from a group of Newcastle miners asking him to investigate a solution to the problem of methane gas which accumulated in the mines, being ignited by the candles the miners wore on their hats. The result, known as the Davy lamp, is his epitaph. In 1818 Davy was made a Baronet, and in 1820 became the president of the Royal Society.

The statue of Humphry Davy looks down Market Jew Street.

THE PILGRIM'S PROGRESS

A walk through the bus terminal will get you onto the path where it follows the line from the train station and into the bay. At low tide it is possible to walk the beach all the way from Penzance and into the harbour at the Mount. At high tide the path still offers great views across the bay as it follows a raised causeway between the beach and the A30. Across this road lies the heliport; another point of departure for those wanting to go to the Scillies. Out in the bay the offshore reefs of the Western Cressar, Cressars and Long Rock are all exposed at low tide and harbour a multitude of wading birds and other shore life. The great arc of sand is well used throughout the year by holiday-makers and locals alike; although the waves are not clean enough to tempt surfers,

Marazion Marshes.

windsurfers nevertheless come here in their droves to make the most of the stiff and steady breezes that sweep across the bay. Other watersport activities include yachting and gig rowing; during the summer months there seems to be a regatta every other week, as hundreds of small dinghies and yachts weave in and out of each other. The sight of so many sails drifting across the water is wonderful, especially when you have the Mount as a backdrop to complete the picture. The Mount's Bay Gig Club is based on the Marazion foreshore and rowers are a regular sight throughout the year out in the bay, fighting against the chop. At the eastern end of the stretch the Red River flows out from the Marazion Marshes and into the sea; the profile of the beach is constantly changing here, as the swell pushes sand up and then back down the beach. The result of this can be to dam the river, creating a freshwater lake which can block your route to Marazion if the tide is high.

Rare birds are most likely to be spotted in the autumn. A lot of migrating birds get blown off course on their travels. Lost, but eager to breed, in desperation most will follow the tail of a depression; as such the days following a spell of bad weather are good times to catch sight of unusual species. Gulls, guillemots, razorbills and fulmars spend the entire winter at sea. Gulls pair for life and return to the same nest site year on year. Seeing rare types of these birds depends on the prevailing wind, but the discovery of a monarch butterfly is a good indicator that rare birds from America are in the area.

This abundance of birds is explained by the presence of the Marazion Marshes, a nature reserve that lies over the Marazion approach road. The area is a honey-pot for twitchers during the migrations; many birds use the marsh as a rest stop before heading north or south, depending on the time of year, and type of bird. Cornwall, especially in the far west, is a haven for the spotter of rare birds. The peninsula lies directly in the flight path of migrating birds coming from the south (Northern Africa) to their breeding grounds in Northern Europe, particularly Scotland and Scandinavia. The most well-known migrants are swallows; they fly during the day, leaving North Africa in February, and always arrive after lunch-time in early April. You never see swallows arrive in the morning, as the final leg of their journey is from France or Spain from where they set out early in the day. Around the middle of October they gather at roost sites in Kenidjack and the Marazion Marshes, as they get ready to fly south again.

During the winter months skylarks can be seen flocking in groups of up to 300. Around the coast path farmers have been encouraged to return to traditional methods of leaving the winter fields as stubble in order to provide feeding grounds for the skylark. This has certainly helped the numbers increase. In the spring Cornwall can boast an average of four or five of these birds per hectare. Hovering over 160ft up, their wondrous song serves as a territorial claim and to attract mates. At night, during the spring months, the distinctive call of the whimbrel may be heard. In winter the curlew has an equally distinctive call. The first cuckoos of the year in Britain can often be heard on the coast path as they are spring arrivals from the south.

The town of Marazion is also known as Market Jew, and people have often thought that this is just an English translation of Marazion. The real reason for the two names is still a matter of conjecture. A reference in 1309 mentions a 'Marcasiou inseta Marcasbygan', implying that there were two habitations adjacent to each other. Throughout Britain, many settlements were born from the charters handed out by the Crown in which the right to hold fairs and markets were granted. This is the case with most of the major settlements in Cornwall and one or two are actually named after the very markets from whence they came. The two small towns of Marcasbygan and Marcasiou, Little Market and Thursday Market respectively, were granted their market charters around 1135. What the settlements were called before then is not known, and the modern form of the towns, Market Jew and Marazion, come from this time. How the two sites were juxtaposed, whether side by side on the mainland or at opposite ends of the causeway, is not known. If it were the latter then the village on the Mount would be Market Jew or Thursday Market with Little Market being on the mainland end of the causeway. The charter in question was granted in connection with the Mount, so the latter seems the more plausible.

It was not until 1595, when Marazion received its charter from Elizabeth I, that the town came to prominence in the bay. Marazion was the first town in West Penwith to receive such a charter, and so started the race between the town and Penzance for superiority and control of trade in the bay. The charter provided Marazion with a Corporation that included a mayor who possessed legal personality and perpetual succession. Organisation of the town prior to the charter constituted a number of burgesses led by a portreeve, and it was not until 1640 that this system was superseded by the Corporation. Members of the Corporation held their posts for life and had the powers to create by-laws and to punish those who transgressed from them. When Penzance was given its charter judicial authority was included and proved to be one of the factors that eventually saw Penzance reign supreme in the struggle for dominance. Pie Powder Courts (a corruption of *pieds pudreux*, meaning 'dusty footed' travellers) were held in Marazion, however, and dealt with disputes arising during fairs. As well as a market on Saturdays two annual fairs were accorded; those of St Barnabas on 11 June and St Andrew on 30 November.

Marazion's position in the bay was strengthened after the Spanish attacked the bay and burned Mousehole, Newlyn and Penzance in 1595. The town was briefly a parliamentary borough and returned two MPs to Richard Cromwell's parliament in 1659 (Richard being the son of Oliver). The population of the town in the seventeenth century was around 1000, which was on a par with Truro, the major town in Cornwall, then as now. The town was largely populated by merchants because of the substantial anchorage at the Mount. They built many of the fine buildings that can still be seen today.

A new wealth, pouring from the tin mines, was beginning to infiltrate the town in the eighteenth century. The beneficiaries became property owners on a grand scale, who required greater mobility to get to and from their mansions around the county. One consequence of this was the 1703 Turnpike Act and the subsequent construction of toll-roads. One of the first in Cornwall ran from Helston through Marazion and ended just outside Penzance. The toll-gate in Marazion stood at the top of the hill close by School Lane; the toll-house has been there since 1781 and the original granite gatepost can still be seen.

The first railway station at Marazion was a typical Victorian affair; timber-built with a slate roof and overhanging canopy. The 317ft platform saw plenty of commercial activity. In fact it was here, rather than Penzance, that the main agricultural exports of the region were loaded for destinations up country. (With only one siding the station handled 3146 tons of potatoes and 3571 tons of broccoli in 1868. This rose to a massive 62 000 tons of spuds and 39 000 tons of broccoli in 1945 when the need for home-grown food was at a peak.)

Even though the station served Marazion, it was still some way from the town, so visitors faced quite a walk or the added expense of a carriage. In October 1903 the first bus service was introduced to accommodate these travellers. The service was later extended to cover St Just and Land's End.

The town was home to its fair share of pubs. Along with those on the Mount which shall be mentioned later, there was, and is, the King's Arms in the middle of town which first opened its doors in the eighteenth century. Up hill is the Fire Engine, named after the first Boulton and Watt engines in Cornwall. The Cutty Sark in the square is another establishment first opened in the eighteenth-century.

The King's Arms public house.

Opposite: *Morning on the sands of Mount's Bay.*

Up Turnpike Lane stands the Sir Christopher Cole School, founded in 1851. At a cost of 1d. per week for each pupil, 100 boys and infants were taught there. Unsurprisingly, absences were common owing to the low income of many. The girls' school on Chapel Street was founded in 1868 on ground adjoining All Saints Chapel.

There are two ways of getting onto the Mount from the mainland, depending on the tide. If it is low then a stroll along the causeway is the done thing. At very low tides it is possible to enter through the harbour. At high tide the only alternative to swimming the expanse, which this book certainly does not recommend, is by water taxi. For about £1 each way this mode of transport is a fun introduction to the secrets of the ancient fortress. The taxi pilots will also, on request, give a circular tour of the island, allowing you to appreciate the extensive grounds at close quarters.

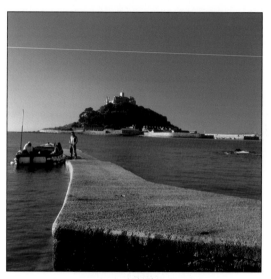

A water taxi waits to leave for the Mount.

The sheltered eastern side of the Mount was undoubtedly the scene of trading between the tin producers and merchants from other parts of Britain and the Continent. Writing in the first century BC the Greek-Sicilian Diodorus Siculus, while on a visit to the far west of Cornwall, remarked that at high tide the Mount (or Ictis, as he called it) appeared to be an island.

The Mount cannot be viewed as either an island or part of the mainland. It is really a tidal island. Its Cornish name is Cara Cowze in Clowze, literally translated as 'the hoar rock in the wood'. This name harks back to the time when forest covered what is now Mount's Bay. The Mount has held a religious significance for the inhabitants of the area for generations. Its origins as a sacred site probably arose from its very geography; Stone, Bronze and Iron Age civilisations always interpreted their surrounding landscape's spiritual significance. High points were usually held as sacrosanct, and used as places of worship, or to bury the dead. For example, the burial chambers on the Isles of Scilly were built on the highest points which protected them from the eventual deluge from the sea. It is more than probable that the early Celtic missionaries contemplated the Mount in the same respect, and in AD495 it is said that a band of fishermen sealed the Mount's fate as a must-visit site for pilgrims when they had a vision of St Michael standing on the rocks on the western side of the island.

After the Norman Conquest, Cornwall was given to Robert, Count of Mortain. He later gave the Mount and half a hide of land (384 acres) to the Benedictine abbey of Mont St Michel in France, which had been built between 1017 and 1144 on the ruins of an earlier church, which stood on the summit. The church was rebuilt in the fourteenth century and a spire was added in the nineteenth. The summit of the Mont rises 400ft above the ocean and commands spectacular views of the surrounding French countryside.

There is much conjecture over the origins of the name St Michael for the Mount. Some say it is due to the French affiliation, others to the vision of the fishermen. Whatever the truth, it was the abbot at Mont St Michael that established the first monastery on the Mount in 1135, and the two island monasteries came to be administered as one body. To enhance the Mount's reputation as a place of pilgrimage, Pope Gregory VII decided that it could confer on all pilgrims, who brought with them alms and oblations, the remission of a third of their penance. This generous offer of salvation still stands to this day, although the alms and oblations now take the form of a £4.50 admission fee to the National Trust.

The meditative life of the monastery continued for almost two centuries. Pilgrims came and went – they were housed, fed, clothed and watered by the villages at either end of the causeway. Business was brisk owing to the fact that the monastery was home to some pretty impressive holy relics: the milk of St Marie the Virgin, the jawbone of St Mansuetus, stones from the Holy Sepulchre, and the pièce de résistance, a fragment of finger bone from St Agapit. Even an earthquake in 1275 that completely destroyed the church, consecrated in 1144, was only a minor interruption to the big business that was absolution.

The Mount at this time could be regarded as a microcosm of Britain in general with religious, mercantile and military life existing in a symbiotic relationship. Its position as a strategically important military stronghold meant the Mount became a theatre of conflict on more than one occasion. In 1193, when Richard I was captured while away on his seemingly never-ending Crusades, his brother John manoeuvred himself onto the throne. The Mount was seized in his name by men disguised as pilgrims. It was held for a year.

The first stone harbour at the Mount was recorded in 1320. A wooden jetty of sorts had, no doubt, existed since the time of Ictis. Penzance and Newlyn were, at this time, nonentities so the Mount was the centre of commerce for the entire bay. The village on the island was not entirely reliant on the monastery for its survival; it was not merely a satellite settlement but rather the major port of entry to the peninsula.

As the Angevin empire slowly receded and England and France became separate realms, the ties between the two monasteries also loosened. The payments made by the Mount to the Mont had always been suspended during times of war, but in 1408 Henry IV diverted them to the English Crown. All links with the monastery on the Mont were severed under Henry V (1413–22).

The two villages at either end of the causeway. The causeway is on the right, partly submerged by the rising tide.

Mount's Bay.

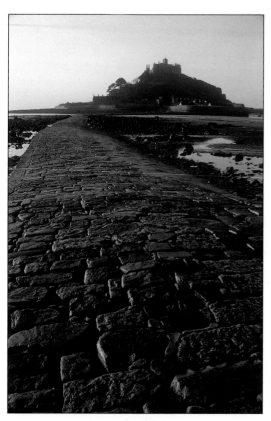

The causeway leading to St Michael's Mount.

As an independent institution the Mount became a transferable asset. It was given by the victor of Agincourt to the newly-established Syon Abbey at Twickenham. Henry VI took it back, however, and affiliated it with his own newly-founded King's College in Cambridge. Syon Abbey was understandably put out at this and, over the next 20 years, fought to recover the Mount, along with its annual income of £3.6s.8d.

At the end of the Wars of the Roses about 80 Lancastrians, headed by the Earl of Oxford, seized the Mount by using the old ruse of dressing as pilgrims. The resulting siege was well defended, partly due to the co-operative policy of the Marazion's sheriff, Sir Henry Bodrugan. Sir John Arundell of Trerice (vice-admiral of Cornwall) was ordered by King Edward IV to recapture it, but was killed on the sands next to the causeway after an altercation. One by one the defenders were lured off the Mount with promises of money and pardon. Oxford, who was running short of men, eventually surrendered to the new sheriff, Richard Fortescue.

The Mount not only fell prey to attackers from home; in 1498 a band of French marauders tried to sack the monastery but failed. In their frustration they torched the village of Marazion before escaping.

In 1539 a thousand years of monastic life came to an end with the nationwide policy of dissolution. From here the Mount took on the role of fortress; defender of the realm rather than the soul. The Mount was leased to the Millington family of Pengersick, with part of the agreement being that they should repair the buildings and maintain a garrison of six soldiers. This was duly done. The life of the soldiers must have been an easy one for the Mount saw little action of note until the Prayer Book Rebellion of 1549. It was with great gusto that the local populace tore through the county in protest at yet another piece of meddling from their 'foreign' overlords. The local gentry were the prime targets of the rebels, and many of them took refuge on the Mount in a bid to save themselves. Another Arundell was the governor of the Mount at the time, as part of his title as Earl of Cornwall, and it was he who led the siege of the Mount. Bales of hay were distributed around the base and set alight in order to create a smoke screen while successive attacks were mounted. The inhabitants eventually surrendered. However, the rebellion itself was soon crushed and Arundell was later hanged at Tyburn for his part in the uprising.

After the Armada was seen off the Lizard in 1588 the Mount's defences were strengthened and a beacon was lit on its summit. Following the destruction of Mousehole, Newlyn and Penzance in the Spanish raids of 1595, Marazion and the Mount once again became the only settlements of any note in the region.

War was a constant drain on the Crown's coffers, and in 1599 the Mount was sold to raise funds. Its new master was Robert Cecil, Earl of Salisbury, who in turn leased it to Sir Robert Harris. The garrison and its defences were kept in good order, but in 1640 the lease was sold to Sir Francis Basset, who later became Sheriff of Cornwall. Basset was one of Charles I's most faithful soldiers and as a result became embroiled in the Civil War. He ensured the safe passage of the Prince of Wales, later Charles II, who reputedly stayed on the Mount, or in Marazion (as well as Sennen don't forget) the night before escaping to the Scillies and on to the Continent.

In 1646 the Royalists surrendered at Truro but General Hopton, the Royalist commander in the region, refused to surrender Pendennis Castle near Falmouth and the garrison on the Mount. He ordered 200 men under Arthur Basset, (brother of Francis) to defend the Mount at all costs. Arthur, however, knew when he was fighting a lost cause and judiciously negotiated a surrender. The Parliamentarians appointed John St Aubyn as Master of the Mount in 1659, and he later purchased it. His occupancy survived the Restoration and the family remain the custodians to this day.

High tide in the harbour.

The St Aubyns lived the life of typical country gentlefolk, with careers in government or the military. They still lived on the family estate at Clowance near Camborne, but this was jeopardised by the fifth baronet who was a bit of a rogue and drank, womanised, fathered 15 illegitimate children – admittedly most to the same local girl whom he later married – and accumulated many debts which nearly ruined the family. Still, they survived to guide the Mount through its next turbulent period: the Napoleonic Wars. The renewed tension in Britain meant that defences were being strengthened all round the coasts and the Mount was no exception. Years earlier one of its garrison guns had been fired at Irish privateers harrying a brig in the bay, but as a result of prolonged inactivity, the gun exploded killing a young soldier. Consequently it was fortunate that when, in 1812, a French frigate was forced aground it had on board some new cannons; these now sit on the Mount's upper terraces.

In 1892 Marazion became a parish town in its own right, one of the smallest in the country. By then Penzance had the industrial supremacy and Newlyn the fishing trade, but Marazion's fate was sealed by the recently established railway which bypassed the town. It was ultimately consigned to the role of gentle resort, which it still holds today. The village on the Mount gave up all pretensions of self-sufficiency and became a model estate, whose existence relied on serving the needs of the St Aubyns.

Towards the end of the Victorian era Sir John St Aubyn, under his new title

Old Cornish cross on St Michael's Mount.

The Mount from Turnpike Lane.

St Michael's Mount.

of Lord St Levan, commissioned his cousin Piers to build a stately home on the Mount. A tunnel was dug to contain a service tramway. A model dairy, a copy of that at Glastonbury, was established in 1870 to serve the island's herd of six Jersey cows. The new estate was praised as an outstanding piece of architecture, in keeping with the already extant buildings. The causeway was built in 1898, but by then the Mount was once more in the throes of a downturn and the ancient rabbit warren and the herd of cows were eventually removed. The Mount was finally given to the National Trust in the 1950s by the St Aubyns, along with a hefty endowment to pay for its upkeep. The family retained the Victorian wing and some of the gardens on a 999-year lease. The tour of the fortress/mansion/monastery is well worth the fee, and allows you to take a leisurely stroll around the grounds.

PATHWAY TO THE FUTURE

So the odyssey is over. There is, of course, nothing to stop you continuing on your walk, but for this book the Mount marks the end. The peninsula around which we have walked plays host to the vestiges of long-extinct civilisations, and it exhibits the scars of some harsh economic truths. Nevertheless, the vitality of the place lies in the fact that the monuments to its yesteryears – the quoits, menhirs, ancient villages, engine houses and factories – all remain in situ. They are trashed only by the very elements that forged their surroundings, and not the rampage of 'progress' that has seen so many similar sites elsewhere in Britain flattened, buried and lost.

We pay homage to the tenacity of the people who created them, who against all the odds burgeoned and flourished to make their indelible mark on the world. The remains of Cornwall's industrial, maritime and cultural past should not be viewed with a heavy heart, in anger at a cruel modern reality, but with joy in the knowledge that when the time was right, the challenges were met.

The region is by no means a museum either. It is true that Cornwall's economy relied on most of the industries that have taken such a hammering over the past fifty years, but it is not a despondent place, inhabited by a whining population, pathetically weeping their plight. The resilience of the Cornish finds a metaphor in the granite from which they built their homes.

The EU has finally recognised the need for reinvestment in Cornwall, and the Objective One money it has given to the region is slowly beginning to filter down to those who need it most. Government at home is also beginning to wake up to the fact that a large proportion of the properties in the county are empty for most of the year; used only as holiday lets and summer retreats for wealthier people up country. Keeping communities together is paramount if Cornwall is to make the most of any opportunities that arise.

From where the renaissance will come is still being decided, but it will come. The tales of heroism, ingenuity and sheer bloody-mindedness that spew forth from the coves, mines and villages along the coast path paint a picture of a people not easily disheartened by onerous circumstances.

New beginnings: the Eden Project by night.

SELECTED BIBLIOGRAPHY

Alcan and Smith. *RNLI St Ives Past, Present, Future*, St Ives Publishing, 1995.

Bird, Sheila. *Mayday: Preserving Life from Shipwreck off Cornwall*, Ex Libris Press, 1990.

Blight, J.T. *A Week at the Land's End*, Alison Hodge, 1989.

Cross, Tom. *The Shining Sands: Artists in Newlyn and St Ives 1880–1930*, Halsgrove, 1999.

Cross, Tom. *Painting the Warmth of the Sun: St Ives Artists 1939–1975*, Halsgrove, 1995.

Cross, Tom. *Catching the Wave: Contemporary Art and Artists in Cornwall*, Halsgrove, 2002.

Curin, John. *Sennen Cove and Its Lifeboat*, nd.

Gendall, Christine. *Porthgwarra*, Churchtown Technology, 1999.

Hedges, E.S. *Tin In Social And Economic History*, Edward Arnold Ltd.

John, C.R. *The Saints Of Cornwall*, Lodenek Press, 1991.

Orme, Nicholas. *Lives Of The Saints: Cornwall and Devon*, Devon & Cornwall Record Society, 1989.

Payne, Robin and Lewsey Rosemarie. *The Romance Of The Stones*, Alexander Associates, 2001.

Pearce, John. *The Wesleys In Cornwall*, D. Bradford Barton Ltd, 1984.

Sagar-Fenton, Michael. *Penlee: The Loss Of A Lifeboat*, Bossiney Books, 1991.

Sinclair, David J. *St Just Mining Area*, Truran, 1987.

Stanier, Peter. *South West Granite*, Cornish Hillside Publications, 1999.

Symons, Alison. *Tremedda Days: A View Of Zennor 1900–1944*, Tabb House, 1992.

Waugh, Mary. *Smuggling In Devon And Cornwall*, Countryside Books, 1992.

Weatherhill, Graig. *Belerion*, Halsgrove, 1998.

Weatherhill, Graig, *Cornovia*, Halsgrove, 1998.

Perry, Margaret E. *Newlyn: A Brief History*, privately published, 1999.

The First and Last, Sennen.